Satan in the Bible,
God's Minister of Justice

(integrity)

p 38

*Th. Temptation of
Jesus*

*To Weed out the phonies—
who don't really believe—*

Mt. 25

*of God they had given to everything
he if both, but he decide to Support maybe
both the J Love seed
elsewhere*

plays may note?

Satan in the Bible, God's Minister of Justice

𖤣

HENRY ANSGAR KELLY

CASCADE *Books* • Eugene, Oregon

SATAN IN THE BIBLE, GOD'S MINISTER OF JUSTICE

Cascade Books
An Imprint of Wipf and Stock Publishers
199 W. 8th Ave., Suite 3
Eugene, OR 97401

www.wipfandstock.com

PAPERBACK ISBN: 978-1-5326-1331-9
HARDCOVER ISBN: 978-1-5326-1333-3
EBOOK ISBN: 978-1-5326-1332-6

Cataloguing-in-Publication data:

Names: Kelly, Henry Ansgar.
Title: Satan in the Bible, God's minister of justice / Henry Ansgar Kelly.
Description: Eugene, OR: Cascade Books, 2017.
Identifiers: ISBN 978-1-5326-1331-9 (paperback) | ISBN 978-1-5326-1333-3 (hardcover) | ISBN 978-1-5326-1332-6 (ebook)
Subjects: LCSH: Devil biblical teaching | Bible. Gospel criticism, interpretation, etc. | Antichrist
Classification: BS2555.6.D5 K25 2017 (print) | BS2555 (ebook)

Manufactured in the U.S.A.   JANUARY 16, 2018

For Sarah and Dominic

What's puzzling you is the nature of my game.

—MICK JAGGER AND KEITH RICHARDS
Sympathy for the Devil

Table of Contents

interesting

Introduction

Introduction

A. Major thesis

Satan in the Bible is not a rebel but God's employee

Over the years I have produced several accounts of the figure of
Satan, correcting or clarifying other accounts, I hope, but always
stressing a central thesis:

There is no basic difference between the presentations of Satan in the Old and New Testaments. He appears as an adversary to
humans, but not to God. Rather, he functions on behalf of God in
various areas of law enforcement, including investigation, intervention, accusation, prosecution, and punishment.

Satan, as I see him, is working for the celestial government,
and perhaps the closest analogue to his position in the American
system is the post of Attorney General. But he is a very unpopular
person, and he is denigrated in various ways in many of the passages of Holy Writ in which he makes an appearance. His motives
and methods appear to be base and immoral, but his ultimate goal
is on the side of the angels: to weed out all unworthy persons from
God's favor. He is deeply suspicious of mortals, and resorts to un-
derhanded tricks to smoke out their true characters. He often fits
the classic definition of an *agent provocateur*: "a person employed,
especially by a government, to induce or incite others to violence
or illegal acts, in order to secure an arrest or discredit a cause."

In other words, I maintain, the character of Satan in the Bible
is quite different from the usual idea of Satan as an enemy of God,
a vengeful creature intent on corrupting virtuous human beings

and thus depriving them of salvation in God's kingdom. The scriptural Satan wants to keep bad people out. The Satan of tradition wants to make good people bad. /

But in spite of the stress that I have laid on this point in my writings, it has not been taken note of or adduced as a position worthy of discussion, let alone of acceptance. One reason may be that it has got lost among peripheral findings in my studies, since it is not emphasized in their titles. My first book, for instance, is called *The Devil, Demonology, and Witchcraft*, or, in the British version, *Towards the Death of Satan* (1968). My most recent book is *Satan; A Biography* (2006). A recent article is "Adam Citings before the Intrusion of Satan" (*Biblical Theology Bulletin*, 2014). The closest I have come to enunciating my main thesis in a title is, "Satan the Old Enemy: A Cosmic J. Edgar Hoover," but it appeared in a rather odd locale, the *Journal of American Folklore* (1990), hardly a mainstream publication.

I have decided, therefore, to produce this book with the title *Satan in the Bible, God's Minster of Justice*. I pray that it works!

B. Common satans and Satan proper

The Hebrew word *satan* is a common noun meaning "adversary" or "opponent," and it is always used in that way in the Hebrew books of the Old Testament. But, as will be explained in chapter 6, the Jews eventually came to think of God as having a particular angel dedicated to "satanic" or adversarial activities or strategies aimed at keeping humans in line. When the Greek-speaking Jews of Egypt translated the books of Job and Zechariah, they considered the generic "satan" of each to be a proper name, Satan, that is, the same "person" in both cases. In Greek they rendered the word with the common noun *diabolos*, "adversary," but treated it as a proper name, *Diabolos*, that is, "Devil," not "a devil." In the "intertestamental" books in Aramaic, Satan becomes Satanah, rendered into Greek as Satanas, which is used in the New Testament, along with Diabolos, to refer to Satan/Devil.

The point of *Diabolos* as a proper name is obscured in English, which conventionally speaks of "the devil," as if this were *not* a proper name, even though in the New Testament it is used only of one person: namely, Satan. In my biography of Satan, I dealt with this problem by referring to "the Devil" in small caps, DEVIL, imitating references to Yahweh as "the LORD." In this present book, I still leave out the definite article "the," but abandon the small caps; I also feel free to refer to "Satan" even where the biblical passages use "Devil."

Abbreviations

LXX	Septuagint
NAB	*Holy Bible: New American Bible*, rev. ed. 2011 (Old Testament 2001)
NIV	*New International Version* (1984)
NJB	*New Jerusalem Bible* (1985)
NOAB	*The New Oxford Annotated Bible*, 4th ed. (2010)
NRSV	New Revised Standard Version (1989)
PG	*Patrologia Graeca*
PL	*Patrologia Latina*
REB	*Revised English Bible* (Oxford 1989; revision of *New English Bible* 1970)

PART 1

The older Old Testament

The Evil One?

Chapter 1

David and other human satans

I want to open my discussion by giving an account of satans who are adversaries or enemies only on the human level. But first let me talk a bit about the nature of the Hebrew Scriptures and its writers.

As is clear even from a superficial reading of the Hebrew Bible, it is made up of a series of what we might call pamphlets, or booklets, which were originally individual scrolls. In fact the Greek word from which "bible" comes is *biblia*, meaning "books," in the plural. But it has long been clear that each booklet is also often a composite of various pieces that have been stitched together or added to. One original writer refers to God (Elohim), while another uses God's personal name, Yahweh. Some scholars have recently tried to identify an active editor or interpolator at the time of the Babylonian Exile—say around 560 BC—to whom they have given the name of "Deuteronomistic Historian," a cumbersome term that we can shorten to "DH."

DH's interventions have been perceived in the four books of Kings, which I will refer to, as usual nowadays, as 1–2 Samuel and 1–2 Kings instead of 1–4 Kings.

One place where DH's hand has been perceived is in 1 Samuel 27–29, a different account of young David's experiences among the Philistines from that which was originally given in chapter 21. In the earlier account, when David fled to King Achish of Gath, the king's servants realized that he was the famous Hebrew warrior. Fearing for his life, David pretended to be mad and thereby made his escape (1 Sam 21:10–15). The new story has it that David and his troops went to King Achish and became his vassals, since the king felt confident that David had turned on his own people. But eventually the Philistine commanders made objection to his presence in their army and demanded that Achish get rid of him: "Send him away, back to his old assignment! Let him not go down with us into battle, because if he does he may become an adversary (*satan*) to us when we fight. What better way to buy back his own king's favor than with the heads of our men?" (1 Sam 29:4).[1]

In this case the satan is conceived of as a military opponent, but seemingly one who is at first undercover and only comes out into the open in a treacherous way. From what we have been told earlier—that David only pretended to Achish that he was being disloyal to Israel (1 Sam 27:8–12)—the Philistine commanders were undoubtedly correct in their assessment.

Later in the life of David another kind of satan appears, seemingly in a passage also authored by DH. After David took over as king, his son Absalom rebelled against him, forcing him to abandon Jerusalem and go on the run. When he was passing through Bahurim, a man named Shemei from the house of Saul started to hurl invectives against him, saying that Yahweh had avenged the blood of Saul on him. Taking the assault as divinely inspired, David refused to allow his men to harm Shimei (2 Sam 16:5–12). Later, after Absalom was defeated, Shimei came and begged forgiveness. David's nephews, sons of his sister Zeruya, then urge him to put Shimei to death for having ridiculed him, who was Yahweh's anointed king. But instead, David forgives him and rebukes his kinsmen: "What is it you do to me today? You have become like satans to me! [literally, "as a satan"]. Should anyone be killed in Israel on this day? Am I not assured of being king of Israel?" (2 Sam 19:22).

Here we see satans as those who attempt to prevent one from acting in accord with one's better nature or duty. It is time for David to show himself magnanimous and merciful, and those who oppose him are to be reprimanded. It is noteworthy that when

---

1. Unless otherwise noted, all scriptural translations are mine.

David comes to the end of his life, he regrets his oath not to harm Shimei, and, without needing any satan to urge him on, he passes a death sentence on Shimei, to be carried out after David dies (1 Kgs 2:8–9).

The next references to satans occur after Solomon succeeds David as king. First, at the beginning of his reign, he summons the architect Hiram and says to him: "You know that my father David could not build a house to the Name of Yahweh his God because of the warfare of those around him, until Yahweh put them under his feet. But now Yahweh my God has given me peace: there is no satan around me, and no disasters" (1 Kgs 5:3–4). Here the term refers to the wagers of war.

But later on, we are told that Yahweh becomes angry with Solomon because of his sins and raises up a satan against him in the person of Hadad the Edomite (1 Kgs 11:14). Hadad was one of the few males of Edom who escaped the slaughter ordered after David's conquest of Edom; he had fled to Egypt, and returned in strength after David's death.

Before hearing any more about Hadad, we are immediately told that God raised up Rezon, son of Eliada, as a satan against Solomon (1 Kgs 11:23). Rezon was the leader of a bandit group that took over Damascus. His life is summed up as a perpetual satan, fomenting the same sort of opposition as the other satan, Hadad: "He was satan to Israel all the days of Solomon, adding to the troubles caused by Hadad; he despised Israel and reigned over Aram" (1 Kgs 11:25).

The important thing to note about these satans is that they are expressly designated as instruments of divine punishment for sins, punishment that falls on the country as a whole, not just on the head of the sinner.

Chapter 2

God Himself as a satan against Balaam

It seems that the Deuteronomistic Historian's hand is to be credited with introducing another satan in the book of Numbers, this time on the angelic and even divine level. The original episode comes just after the business about the poisonous serpents in the desert. The Israelites are near the end of their forty-year sojourn. As a punishment for their complaining, Yahweh sends an infestation of serpents, which kills many people. Eventually, Yahweh instructs Moses to set up a bronze replica of a serpent, which has the effect of curing the snakebite of anyone who looks at it (Num 21:5–9). After many battles with local peoples along the King's Highway through Transjordan, the Israelites settle on the plains of Moab, across the Jordan from Jericho.

Balak, the king of the Moabites, is greatly concerned about the invaders and their military prowess and sends a delegation to employ the services of a prophet named Balaam to utter maledictions against them. Balaam himself is willing enough, but insists that he must first obtain Yahweh's permission. God (Elohim) comes that night to Balaam and asks him who these emissaries are. When Balaam tells Him that the Moabite king wishes his help to drive out the new arrivals, God refuses to allow him to go with them because these people are under His protection. When the Moabites persist, Balaam seeks further instructions, and this time God agrees that he should go with them, but he is to speak out only in the manner that God will show him. Accordingly, Balaam

6

mounts his jenny (female donkey) and sets out with his guides (Num 22:1–21).

Then another author, likely DH (because of his affinity for satans), created a new account of the same episode; but rather than deleting or revising the original story, he simply set it next to it, and started the tale over again. He takes up with Balaam on the donkey, but now it is as if Balaam had never broached his mission with God and had never been given permission to go. In fact, we are told, "Balaam's departure aroused the anger of Yahweh, and the Angel of Yahweh stood in the road as a *satan* against him" (Num 22:22). "Angel of Yahweh" should doubtless be translated as something like "manifestation of Yahweh," because when the figure speaks, it is with the words of Yahweh Himself.

While in the earlier account Balaam is traveling with the Moabite men, in this new narrative, he has two of his own servants with him on foot. Despite the presence of these potential witnesses, we are told that only the donkey can see the satan, sword in hand, standing in the road before her, and she suddenly bolts off into the field next to the road. When Balaam, disconcerted, beats her back to the path, the armed figure no longer blocks the way, but, sure enough, appears again, and the jenny now swerves into a vineyard wall, injuring Balaam's foot. More beating ensues, but the angel has by now disappeared, so they get under way again. This time, when the angel reappears, there is no room on either side of the road, so the jenny can only collapse on the spot. Balaam then starts to lay into her with a will, when, startlingly, empowered by the angel, she begins to speak, and rebukes Balaam: "Why have you beat me these three times, what harm have I done to you?" Balaam responds, "You are making a fool of me—if I had my sword with me I would have killed you!" The donkey replies, "Why, haven't I carried you faithfully all these years? Have I ever caused you any trouble like this before?" Balaam, seeing her point, readily admits that she is right. "No," he says.

We might expect that now the donkey will explain what the problem is, but Yahweh or His angel decides that enough is enough, and finally makes Himself seen with sword in hand, standing there in the road before Balaam. He says, "Why have you beat your ass these three times? She saw me coming against you as a satan to stop you from going forward, because your journey is foolhardy. She saw me, and turned away three times, saving your life. If she had not done so, I would have killed you and spared her." Balaam, aghast, hurries to prostrate himself on the ground, admitting his sin: "I did not know you were standing there to oppose me. Since it is against your will, I will go back." But, surprisingly, the Angel of Yahweh relents and gives him permission to proceed: "Go with these men, but speak only what I will tell you" (Num 22:22–35).

The whole episode, especially taken in conjunction with the original sober account, seems like a comedy of errors, with Yahweh's satanic opposition completely uncalled for and blunderingly executed. But the basic meaning of *satan* is clear: an agent of obstruction, here obviously in a good cause, since God himself in effect acts as the satan, instead of, as in the books of Kings, instigating human satans as obstructions against those men who needed to be obstructed.

Chapter 3

God and a heavenly satan confer about Job

The book of Job is a strange account of a holy man who is not Jewish. The body of the work, chapters 3 to 42, is in verse, whereas the first two chapters constitute a prose Prologue, with the last half of chapter 42 also in prose, functioning as an epilogue. It is the Prologue we are interested in, dealing as it does with another supernatural satan. Some scholars see it as imitating the Deuteronomistic Historian's use of "satan," therefore dating it around 550 BC.

The Prologue begins an account of an upright man named Job in the land of Uz, who, we are told, feared God, adhering only to what was good and shunning all wrongdoing. Then comes an account of Yahweh in His heavenly court as His angels arrive, to report on their activities. They are called "sons of God" (Job 1:6), and one of them is a *satan*. Yahweh addresses only the satan, and asks for an accounting. The satan announces that he has been on his usual patrols, "going back and forth upon the earth," observing the doings of human beings (Job 1:7, 2:2). Yahweh is particularly interested in one of his favorite people, Job, whom he calls His servant, praising him as the most upright man in the world—and naturally expecting a favorable report. But the satan surprises Him, by calling Job's virtue into question and in need of testing. According to the satan, the only reason Job is so admirable is that Yahweh has given him all that he needs and protected him from all adversities: "It is not for nothing that he is a God-fearing man. Have you not put a wall around him and all he possesses? You have

9

blessed all of his endeavors and multiplied his livestock across the plains. But reach out and strike it all down, and you will see him blaspheme you to your face!" (Job 1:9–11).

Yahweh agrees to let the satan destroy all of Job's possessions, but He also participates in the onslaught, because one of the disasters that happens, the destruction of his flocks of sheep, is caused by "God's fire" (Job 1:16), that is, thunderbolts, but obviously called up at the satan's command, like the tornado that later kills Job's children. The satan has also been able to organize human marauders to come and kill his servants and carry off his oxen, donkeys, and camels. However, Job, who knows nothing of the satan, and considers it all the doing of Yahweh, remains unshaken in his devotion: "Yahweh gave, and Yahweh has taken back, blessed be the name of Yahweh!" (Job 1:21).

At the next gathering of the sons of God before Yahweh, Yahweh again immediately singles out the satan for his report on his earthly patrols. As before, Yahweh both asks after and praises Job, and then He Himself reports on the outcome of their testing: "He is still upright in his virtue, even though you incited me against him to ruin him without reason" (Job 2:3).

This is remarkable: Yahweh acknowledges that the satan tempted Yahweh Himself to do the wrong thing, to act against Job without reason, and that he succeeded; Yahweh succumbed to the temptation. The satan then proceeds to repeat the feat, and again gains permission to lash out against Job, this time by afflicting his very body.

Satan urges the action in a highly rhetorical way, shouting "Skin for skin!"—meaning, "Attack his body!"—not just his goods. "Strike his flesh and bones, and you can be sure that he will curse you to your face!" (Job 2:4–5). Yahweh gives in: "Very well, then, do what you want, only do not kill him" (Job 2:6). After horrific skin infections are inflicted upon Job, Job's wife succumbs to the trial, telling Job to curse God and die, but Job remains steadfast.

There is no return to the super-setting of the story. We are only told at the end that Yahweh restored Job's prosperity twofold, while his brothers and sisters and former friends, giving him money and jewelry, consoled him for all of the evil that Yahweh (and not the satan) had brought upon him (Job 42:11).

The author of the Prologue to Job, writing a prequel to the already existing dialogues of the suffering Job and his so-called consolers, may have been inspired by some elements in these original exchanges. For instance, Yahweh's rebuke to the satan, for making Him harm Job for no good reason, may be a reflection of Eliphaz's assertions that God finds fault even with His angels (Job 4:18), that God does not trust even the sons of God, and that the very heavens are not clean in His sight (Job 15:15).

As we will see below, the satan will become "Satan" (that is, a specific angel named Satan), and his negotiations with the Lord over Job will remain paradigmatic for the rest of his biblical career in the New Testament. From a moral standpoint, neither God nor Satan wins high marks of character.   *true*

The next Life - Justice.

But God did not even
Spare Jesus, his own Son.

Chapter 4

Heavenly and human satans as judicial prosecutors against humans: Zechariah 3 and Psalm 109

We see another kind of celestial satan in the book of Zechariah, the eleventh of the twelve Minor Prophets, a book that begins in the year 519 BC, that is, some time after the Israelites have returned to Jerusalem from their exile in Babylon. It consists of a series of visions, the first of which reminds us of the book of Job, because it concerns angels who patrol the earth. But unlike the satan of Job, these angels are on horseback, and their function seems quite different. They report to another horseman (who turns out to be the Angel of Yahweh) that the whole earth is finally at peace. Then in an unusual development, since the Angel of Yahweh often speaks with the voice of Yahweh Himself, the Angel addresses Yahweh: "How long will you refuse to have mercy on Jerusalem and its cities? Your anger has lasted these seventy years." Yahweh replies, "I will return to Jerusalem with mercy and there my house will be rebuilt. . . . I will again choose Jerusalem" (Zech 1:8–17).

More visions follow, foretelling Jerusalem's glorious future, and then the scene shifts to heaven. The realm of Yahweh now functions as a judicial court, complete with celestial prosecutor, human defendant, and judge. The prosecutor's role is taken by a *satan*, but, contrary to the precedent set in the Numbers story of Balaam, where the Angel of Yahweh played the role of a satan, here the Angel of Yahweh assumes what might at first appear to us as

12

a defense attorney's position, until it turns out that he is in charge of the whole proceedings: that is, he is the judge. It is another angel who is the satan, as in the book of Job, now taking the role of prosecutor.

The defendant is Joshua, the current High Priest in Jerusalem, who is obviously guilty as charged—whatever the charges are—because he appears dressed in filthy garments. The text reads: "Then he showed me the High Priest Joshua, standing before the Angel of Yahweh, with a satan standing at his right side making accusations against him" (Zech 3:1). Whereupon, without proceeding further in the case, even to hear a plea from the accused, the judge enters a definitive sentence in his favor, perhaps also asserting malfeasance on the part of the prosecutor. We guess that this is true, because the Angel of Yahweh calls on Yahweh Himself to reprimand the satan: "May Yahweh rebuke you, satan!" (Zech 3:2).

According to this angel, the high priest merits absolution because he must be rescued from his abject condition before it is too late. He demands of the satan, "Is not this man like a burning branch snatched from the fire?" (Zech 3:2).

The Angel of Yahweh then rehabilitates Joshua on the spot. He directs his attendants to remove his encrusted clothing and to put on a clean set of priestly robes. He tells Joshua: "Behold, I have removed all of your sins and guilt from you" (Zech 3:4). He then conveys Yahweh's message to Joshua and also those who are standing there, that is, Joshua's priestly colleagues, who are awaiting trial as well. Joshua will have full access to Yahweh's house and courts, and eventually Yahweh will remove all the guilt from all the people on a single day (Zech 3:6–9).

* * *

There is another Scripture in which a satan appears as a judicial prosecutor, namely, Psalm 109. It is a typical "cursing psalm," one in which the speaker rails against his enemies, and asks God to punish them mercilessly. In this case, the psalmist opens by complaining that he is the constant object of hateful lies: "Wicked

13

and deceitful mouths shout against me, speaking out with lying tongues." He says, rather unconvincingly, that he has loved these people, but they returned hatred for his love, and evil for the good that he has done to them. He goes on at length to illustrate their evildoings in their own words: "Let us appoint an evil judge in his case, and a *satan* at his side to accuse him. Let a guilty verdict be given at his trial, with his pleas of innocence turned against him" (Ps 109:6–7).

After a long set of other unspeakable disasters wished down upon him by his tormentors, the psalmist calls them all *satans* and prays that Yahweh will visit such calamities upon them as punishment for their enmity; he then begs that every one of those who "satanize" against him will be put to shame (Ps 109:20, 29).

PART 2

The Newer Old Testament

Chapter 5

A human satan causes David's sin in Chronicles

After witnessing a variety of human and heavenly satans at work in the Old Testament, we come to a case in Chronicles, where the satan's exact sphere, human or angelic, is disputed. Scholars also dispute the Chronicler's time and years of activity, dating him from the sixth century BC to as late as the third or even second century BC. For myself, I argue below that the satan in question is a human adversary; and I also think that the work was written comparatively late; therefore I here place this chapter in the "newer Old Testament."

The Chronicler's purpose was to rework the books of Samuel and Kings. But unlike the Deuteronomistic Historian, who added new material without replacing the old, even when his additions contradicted the original narrative, the Chronicler felt free to eliminate sections that would interfere with his themes—for instance, his presentation of a completely sinless and moral Solomon.

Let us look first at the passage in 2 Samuel into which the Chronicler will insert a satan. It comes at the end of the book, the last of a series of miscellaneous episodes tucked in to finish off the history, and it tells of a strange offense committed by David upon deliberate provocation by Yahweh Himself. The section begins, "Again the anger of Yahweh was aroused against Israel, and He incited David against them" (2 Sam 24:1).

The crime consisted of David's taking a census of his people—previously not a crime at all, but a divine requirement, as witnessed

17

by the "book of Censuses," that is, Numbers. After David succumbed, Yahweh gave him the choice of three punishments: three years of famine, three months of harassment by his enemies, or three days of pestilence. He chose the last, and so the Angel of Yahweh, acting as a destroying angel, killed off 70,000 of David's subjects by "stretching out his hand," doubtless a sword-bearing hand. When he came to ravage Jerusalem, Yahweh relented and commanded him to stay his hand, saying, "It is enough" (2 Sam 24:16).

But what follows gives a contradictory story: when David sees the angel who was destroying his people, he prays to Yahweh for mercy, pleading that his people should not be punished for a sin that is his doing alone. It is only now (not earlier) that Yahweh will stop the slaughter, after David performs an elaborate sacrifice, as demanded (2 Sam 24:25).

Let us see now what the Chronicler makes of this story: he starts out by saying, not that it was the anger of Yahweh that caused David to commit his sin, but rather a *satan*, who stood up against Israel and incited David to number his subjects (1 Chr 21:1).

Whether the Chronicler is speaking here of a human or a heavenly satan, it is certain that he knows about human satans, for he saw such satans earlier in Samuel and made a point of eliminating them in his rewrite: specifically, where David is called a satan (1 Sam 29:4), and where David calls his kinsmen satans for advising him to break his vow about Shimei (2 Sam 19:22). In condensing the books of Kings, he will go on to eliminate the satans Haddad and Rezon whom God had raised up against Solomon (1 Kgs 11). Therefore it is not only plausible but even probable that he invented a human satan to cause David's sin of census-taking, in order to take possible opprobrium away from Yahweh, thereby relieving Him of the awkward moral position of forcing David to sin.

If, on the other hand, we should wish to see a heavenly satan here, it would have the effect of compounding Yahweh's "guilt" for His actions. While it could readily be conceded that His renewed anger against Israel was justified, since the Israelites were notorious for stepping out of line and offending Him, still, to force his servant David, the anointed king of His people, to commit a sin, in order to justify His punishing of David's subjects, would fall well below expected divine standards. And for an angel to play the role of the inciting satan would only compound the problem, since the celestial satan would naturally be taken to be acting at Yahweh's behest. Furthermore, the Chronicler does not mention the original motivation, Yahweh's anger against the offending Israelites.

One reason why most modern interpreters have been too quick to see a supernatural satan here, and even a figure with the proper name of Satan, is that it was long customary to consider the satans of Job and Zechariah as "evil" altogether, and in all likelihood influenced by the Persian concepts of Zoroaster, that is, a good god, Ahura Mazda, balanced by an evil god, Angra Mainyu. But more recently, exegetes have concluded that any evil that attached to the Old Testament satans was not of the ontological or moral kind, but only on the level of misfortunes arising from divine governance, that is, "natural evils."

Nevertheless, Persian influence should not be discounted altogether when trying to account for the Old Testament satans. It is entirely likely that there was such influence, not however from the religious or philosophical sphere but rather from the administrative or bureaucratic side of things. The royal officials of the Persian kingdom who were in charge of reporting problems in the provinces were called the "eyes and ears of the king." We can easily see how the satan of Job could be related to them, for listen to his two reports to Yahweh. They both have a boilerplate prologue: the satan has come "from going to and fro on the earth, and from walking up and down upon it" (Job 1:7, 2:3).

cf Isa.

19

Chapter 6

The Septuagint (LXX):
Satan proper, and common satans

The Hebrew Scriptures were gradually translated by the Greek-speaking Jews of Egypt over a period of time ranging from the century before to the century after 200 BC. The Greek text is called the Septuagint (abbreviated LXX), and is invaluable in demonstrating how the original Hebrew passages were interpreted at the time of translation. It is also important as the version of the Old Testament that was used and cited by the authors of the New Testament. In addition, we must always be aware of the possibility that it preserves an older or original version of given passages, because the Hebrew text that we now have was fixed much later, around AD 200, by the Masoretic editors.

A) Satan (Devil) is the adversarial angel of Job and Zechariah

On our present subject, the most striking interpretation of the Septuagint is that the satan of Job and the satan of Zechariah are seen to be one and the same angel whose actual name is Satan, but given now in the Greek, *Diabolos*, or, in the English derivative, "Devil."

As noted in the Introduction, we know that "Satan" was also used in Hebrew and in Greek for the name of this adversarial angel because of the Aramaic form *Satanah*, which, as *ho satanas* in

Greek, is used as an alternate name for *ho diabolos* in the New Testament.

The English word "devil" has been treated misleadingly in Bible translations. It should be rendered in the same way as *theos*, "god." When *theos* and *diabolos* do not have a definite article, they should be translated as "god" (plural "gods") and "devil" (plural "devils"). But when the former has an article, *ho theos*, it is properly translated not as "the god" or "the God," but as "God," a proper name. The same should be true for *ho diabolos*; it should not be rendered "the devil" or "the Devil, " but simply "Devil."

The beginning of the celestial passage in the Greek (LXX) text of chapter 1 of Job should be translated like this: "Now it came to pass on a certain day that the angels of God came to stand before the Lord, and Devil came with them. And the Lord said to Devil, 'Where are you coming from?' And Devil answered the Lord and said, 'I have come from going about the earth and walking up and down under heaven,'" and so on.

Many standard translations of the Hebrew text of Job (starting at verse 6) get it wrong in presenting it as already portraying an angel named Satan. For instance, the NRSV (New Revised Standard Version, 1989) has, "One day the heavenly beings came to present themselves before the LORD, and Satan also came among them," etc. The attached note says, "or the Accuser." The capital "A" obviously signifies that this is a unique position filled by a specific angel.

Certain commented editions of the NRSV attempt to explain away the idea of a proper name or a proper noun. For instance, *The New Oxford Annotated Bible*, or *NOAB* (ed. 4, 2010), says that this figure is not the adversary of God, but the adversary of Job and other humans: "He is not the 'devil' of later Jewish and Christian literature."

The *NOAB* is an ecumenical Bible, with largely Catholic commentators. The official American Catholic translation, NAB (*Holy Bible: New American Bible*, rev. ed., 2011 [OT, 2001]) is an improvement on the NRSV: "One day, when the sons of God came to present themselves before the LORD, the satan also came among them." The NAB annotation likens this member of the heavenly court to the human satan of 1 Kings 11:14, and states further, "In later biblical traditions this character will be developed as the devil (Gk *diabolos,* 'adversary')."

The same observations are to be made of Zechariah 3; it is only with the Septuagint that Satan/Devil can be spoken of. In other words, in the Greek translation an angel named Satan/Devil appears in both Job and Zechariah as the celestial functionary who, in the first book, discussed Job with the Lord, and, in the second book, acted as prosecutor in the heavenly court against the high priest, here named "Jesus" (the Greek for Joshua). Now the episode reads, in correct translation: "The Lord showed me the High Priest Jesus, standing before the Angel of the Lord, and Devil stood on his right side to oppose him. And [the Angel of] the Lord said to Devil, 'The Lord rebuke thee, O Devil—the Lord who has chosen Jerusalem rebuke thee!'"

Predictably, standard modern translations of the Hebrew text of Zechariah show the same variation as in Job. The NRSV gets it wrong: "Then he showed me the high priest Joshua standing before the angel of the LORD, and Satan standing at his right hand to accuse him," while the NAB gets it right: "Then he showed me the high priest Joshua standing before the angel of the LORD, while the adversary stood at his right side to accuse him," with a note: "Later tradition understands this figure to be Satan." An earlier Catholic version, the *New Jerusalem Bible* (NJB), puts "Satan" in the translation, with no explanatory note.

But the NJB is more literal in naming "Yahweh" where it occurs in the Hebrew text, rather than substituting "the Lord," a convention that started in the Septuagint. Other English versions of the Old Testament, which ostensibly present the Hebrew text, are misleading in following the Septuagint convention as if it was also the practice of the Hebrew text, telling us only in their prefaces that when "the LORD" appears, in small caps, it means that it is "Yahweh" in the original.

B) Common human devils and satans in the Septuagint

Where else does the Septuagint find Satan? The answer is: nowhere. Everywhere else we find the same sort of common human satans that were in the Hebrew, except in the story of Balaam, where there is paraphrase. Let's look:

Numbers:

The *satan* who figures in the story of Balaam in the book of Numbers is identified as "the Angel of the Lord," and therefore could hardly be Satan. In fact the first instance of *satan* here, instead of being translated *diabolos*, is turned into the related verb, *endiaballein*, "to oppose," and the second instance is rendered with another noun, *diabolē*, "opposition" (LXX Num 22:22, 32).

Chronicles:

As for the *satan* in the Chronicler's account of David and the census, it is rendered *diabolos*, without the article, simply "a devil," that is, "a satan," not Satan. If the translator was alert to the sort of reasoning I gave above, he would consider this devil to be a human adversary, not an angel sent by the Lord.

Samuel:

When they came to the satans of the books of Samuel, the Greek translators did not use *diabolos* but *epiboulos*, meaning "plotter" (LXX 1 Sam 29:4; 2 Sam 19:22).

Kings:

The same term, *epiboulos*, was employed for the statement that there were no satans when Solomon began to rule (LXX 1 Kgs

5:4). But at the point where Yahweh stirred up the satans Hadad and Rezon against Solomon, the Septuagint translators did not translate at all but transliterated the Hebrew word into Greek, *satan*, "satan" (LXX 1 Kgs 11:14, 23). But for the next use of *satan*, in verse 25, another term for opponent was used: *antikeimenos*.

Psalms:

In Psalm 109 (or 108, as it is counted in LXX), where a satan stood against me in the courtroom of my enemies, in the Greek it is a devil, *diabolos*, and the satans or satanizers of verses 20 and 29 are "bedevilers," *endiaballontes*.

In addition, there are three more places in the Greek Bible where new devils appear:

Esther:

In the Hebrew text of Esther, the queen reports to King Ahaserus, "The enemy oppressing us is this wicked Haman" (7:6), rendered much the same in the Greek. But a bit later, where the Hebrew text says that the king "gave the house of Haman, enemy of the Jews, to Queen Esther" (8:1), the Greek says that he "gave to Esther all that belonged to Haman the devil (*diabolos*)."

Maccabees:

After Jerusalem is captured by the invading King Antiochus IV Epiphanes, the city itself becomes an "evil" or "harmful" devil (*diabolos ponēros*) to Israel (1 Macc 1:36).

Wisdom:

We will see in Chapter 8 below that Cain is called an envious devil (Wis 2:24).

Chapter 7

p. 12?
(3/22)

The Genesis prequel:
no satan or Satan in Eden, just the serpent *?*

It is now time to deal with the widespread tradition that Satan made an appearance in the garden of Eden under the form of a serpent.

Let me start by noting that the first eleven chapters of Genesis, which extend from the creation to the tower of Babel, seem clearly to have been a later addition to Genesis, attached as a "prequel" to the story of Abraham, perhaps around 300 BC. *?*

The first chapter deals with the creation of the world in six days, culminating, after the creation of plants, fish, birds, and animals, in the creation of humankind, both men and women. The second chapter tells a contradictory story of creation, with a single man created first, followed by plants and animals, and, finally, a single woman.

The latter story *(p. 2)* goes like this. First, after making the heavens and earth, Yahweh-God created a man, 'adam, and put him in a garden, Eden, which as yet had no plants or animals. He created the plants immediately, including the trees, singling out for mention the tree of life in the middle of the garden, and also the tree *1 Trees?* of knowing good and bad. Adam was forbidden to eat the fruit of the latter tree on pain of instant death ("On the day that you eat of it, you will die the death" [Gen 2:17]). Then, because Yahweh-God realized that it was not suitable for Adam to live by himself, He started to create various animals in the hope of producing a

There a immately
25 *immediately*

suitable companion for him. Each animal was rejected in succession, including, of course, the animal that would be characterized as the cleverest of them all, the serpent. Finally, Yahweh-God produced the woman from the side of the man.

Chapter 3 begins: "Now the serpent was the most knowing of all of the animals of the field that Yahweh-God had made." He approaches the woman, later named Eve, and asks her about the prohibition on eating fruit. He professes to understand it to apply to all of the fruit-bearing trees. She corrects him, telling him that the command referred only to the tree in the middle of the garden: if they ate its fruit, or even touched the tree, they would die. The serpent responds by saying that it is not true what God said. On the contrary, if they ate the fruit, they would not die but would become like God, knowing everything good and bad, and God only forbade it to prevent them from obtaining this knowledge.

After Eve succumbs and eats, and after Adam eats as well, it turns out that what the serpent said was true: they do not die, and they do acquire the divine knowledge of good and bad, as Yahweh-God later confirms (Gen 3:22).

Each of the participants in this misdeed receives a punishment, but none of the three punishments consists of instant death or even eventual death. True, Adam's punishment, difficulty in raising crops, will persist until he returns to the earth, but the reason given for his return to earth is not that he disobeyed the divine command, but rather that the earth is where he came from, like the animals: all will return to it. The serpent, who shares in this fate of returning to the earth, has the punishment of being the most despised of all animals, condemned to crawling on his belly and eating earth as long as he lives (that is, until he returns to earth), and there will be enmity between his offspring and the woman's offspring (Gen 3:14–15).

We can see how the clever talking serpent in Eden could readily have been taken to be acting as a *satan* against Eve by other authors and editors of the Hebrew Scriptures, if only they had known the story. But, since there is no mention at all of the Adam and Eve story after its appearance at the beginning of Genesis, we

[handwritten margin note: Paul believes as Christ. Jesus]

can assume that it was a later invention and addition. The first re-actions to the story occur in the later Greek Scriptures, specifically Tobit and Sirach, but only in terms favorable to the first parents, with no reference to their mishap. (I show this in my article, "Adam Citings before the Intrusion of Satan," mentioned in the Introduction.) For a supposed exception, see the next chapter, on Wisdom.

Meanwhile, let me make the further point that even if the Eden serpent were to be thought of as a common-noun *satan* or *diabolos*, he could hardly be deemed an angelic *satan*, let alone Satan/Devil, seen to be at work in Job and Zechariah, since the serpent is quite clearly said to be one of the animals that Yahweh-God created.

[handwritten notes at bottom of page:]

The origin of
    Conscience
    Conscius

    discretion

Serpent was 'Wise' =
a ekonpenial queir?
man! Enter Enquire

Jesu died on a tree to rev
recover man existive to tru 1 life

Chapter 8

Wisdom's envious devil:
not Satan-serpent, but Cain

I examine now the widespread assumption by biblical translators and commentators that the book of Wisdom, the latest of the
traditional Old Testament books (it is dated variously between 50
BC and AD 50), identifies the serpent who seduced Eve as Satan,
because it is said at one point that death entered the world through
the envy of a *diabolos* (Wis 2:24).

The idea of this interpretation, of course, is that, since God
told Adam that eating the forbidden fruit would bring death, and
since it was the serpent who persuaded Eve to eat it, it follows that
the Wisdom author is calling the serpent a *diabolos*, so why not assume that he was not thinking of a common-noun garden-variety
diabolos, but rather *Diabolos* himself, that is, Satan, who features
in Job and Zechariah?

There are some obvious things wrong with this scenario:

1) To begin with, as we have just seen, God does not carry out
   His threat to impose death as a punishment on Adam and
   Eve.

2) Considering Adam's sin to be so heinous as to bring death into
   the world is at variance with the Wisdom author's extremely
   indulgent idea of Adam's sin as a mere peccadillo, certainly
   not warranting such an extreme punishment.

3) How could a talking animal be construed as one of the angels of the Lord?

4) Apart from the fact that *diabolos* here lacks the requisite definite article indicating a proper name, it would be at variance with the Wisdom author's practice of never using proper names.

The second of these points is by far the strongest objection to this interpretation. All that one has to do is to read on in the book to see what the Wisdom author thinks of Adam. He takes him up in chapter 10, where Adam stands at the head of a series of seven contrasts between a good man and a bad man: Adam being the first good man, and his murdering son Cain being the first bad man. The second good man is Noah, while the second bad man is the same as the first, Cain. Here is the text:

> [Lady Wisdom] protected the first-formed father of the world, when he alone had been created; she delivered him from his transgression, and gave him the strength to rule all things. But when an unjust man departed from her in his anger, he perished because in rage he killed his brother. When the earth was flooded because of him, Wisdom again saved it, steering the just man by a mere piece of wood. (Wis 10:1–4)

We also see in this passage the answer to the question of who the envious *diabolos* is at the end of chapter 2: namely Cain, who was upset when his brother Abel's sacrifice was accepted by the Lord and his own rejected, whereupon in a fit of jealous rage he killed him.

This conclusion was obvious to the first known reader of the book of Wisdom, St. Clement of Rome, honored as the third pope, in the letter that he wrote to the Christians of Corinth. This is what he says:

> Everyone walks after his own wicked lusts, resuming the practice of an unrighteous and ungodly envy, "by which Death himself entered into the World" (Wis 2:24); for thus it is written: "And it came to pass after certain days,

that Cain brought of the fruits of the earth a sacrifice unto God; and Abel also brought of the firstlings of his sheep, and of the fat thereof. And God had respect to Abel and to his offerings, but Cain and his sacrifices He did not regard. And Cain was deeply grieved, and his countenance fell. And God said to Cain, 'Why art thou grieved, and why is thy countenance fallen? If thou offerest rightly, but dost not divide rightly, hast thou not sinned? Be at peace: thine offering returns to thyself, and thou shalt again possess it.' And Cain said to Abel his brother, 'Let us go into the field.' And it came to pass, while they were in the field, that Cain rose up against Abel his brother, and slew him" (Gen 4:3–8). You see, brethren, how envy and jealousy led to the murder of a brother." (Clement, *Epistle to the Corinthians*, 3–4)

It seems clear that the modern interpretation of the *diabolos* as Satan in Eden has been influenced by the prejudice of tradition.

PART 3

The oldest New Testament:
Paul's Epistles

Chapter 9

Introduction to the spirit world
of the New Testament

The spirit world of traditional Christianity is very impoverished, compared to most other traditions and cultures. For most Protestants, it consists only of God, good angels, and fallen angels, called demons or "devils." Angels are entirely good, demons entirely bad. Human souls also persist after death, of course, but they have nothing to do with the world they have left, being consigned permanently to heaven or to hell.

Catholics believe in the same entities, but they also believe that some departed souls are in purgatory and that souls in purgatory or in heaven can make appearances back on earth. When they make such appearances they are not called "ghosts," but either "saints" or "suffering souls."

Even biblical scholars have come to their fields with these inherited mind-sets and must guard against their influence. For instance, a common assumption is that the possessing demons of the Gospels are, if not fallen angels, somehow mini-devils, like their master, Satan. But an objective analysis shows that they are simply parasites in need of "hosts"; their presence causes bodily afflictions, but they have no tempting function—they are not out to corrupt the morals of their hosts. They are like disease germs in being invisible, but unlike them in being rational and able to speak. Satan makes use of them, like other diseases, for his own purposes. We are now about to see what those purposes are. But

33

first we must clear our minds of all preconceptions about him, except for those that we have just garnered from the Old Testament.

The almost universal presumption of biblical exegetes, even those who believe that the satans of the books of Job and Zechariah are not sinful and fallen creatures but rather angels in good standing with God, is that, in the New Testament, Satan (*ho Satanas*), otherwise known as Devil (*ho Diabolos*), is completely different, a thoroughly evil enemy of God and man alike. They can offer no explanation for how this came about, because the old story of Lucifer's rebellion and fall is no longer intellectually respectable. At most, they can only make vague allusions to the likelihood of Zoroastrian influences on the Jews, perhaps pointing to the Angel of Darkness or Belial of the Dead Sea Scrolls. But these figures are not like Satan, in that they are inert "personifications without personality."

Aside from the fact that there is no proof for Zoroastrian dualistic influence on the Jews, there is no need for it, if the presupposition of Satan's radically evil nature is discarded. If he appears to grow in malevolence, it can be readily explained internally, from naturally building resentment against him. We must always take note where his malevolence, that is, his "ill-will," is directed: namely, to humankind. Why is it not possible for one of God's good angels to be in a bad mood now and then, or to have a bias against certain persons, or to be guilty of brutal or unfair tactics, while still performing his basic duties as an overseer of humankind?

We might be tempted to answer that God would not permit such behavior. But who are we to judge? God himself often exhibits similar behavior in the pages of the Old Testament, becoming wrathful and unreasonable and indulging in genocidal overkill.

Let us listen to the authors of the New Testament books, who were free to say anything they liked about both God and Satan. Because Satan was off to a bad start to begin with, having a name that means "adversary," it is not surprising that other bad things were attributed to him in written accounts. That is the way the media work today, and that is the way they have always worked.

All this is prologue to my reminding readers that no one, to my knowledge, has entertained or even noticed my thesis that the Satan/Devil of Job and Zechariah, as presented in the Septuagint, is almost exactly the same character as the Satan/Devil of the New Testament, except for individual variations of each author, or each book, in the canon. It is my goal to summarize and discuss all of those variations in the pages that follow.

Isa. 30+

Chapter 10

Paul's Satan as opposer: testing, punishing, rehabilitating: 1 Thessalonians and 1 Corinthians

We begin with the earliest writings of the earliest author of the New Testament, Paul of Tarsus. Some of the letters attributed to him (that is, which are written in his name) are not by him at all in the opinion of most scholars nowadays. An example is the Second Letter to the Thessalonians, which begins: "Paul, Silvanus, and Timothy, to the church of the Thessalonians in God our Father and the Lord Jesus Christ." We will deal with it and others like it below, as authored by "Pseudo-Paul" or "Deutero-Paul."

Meanwhile, we will start with 1 Thessalonians, which is acknowledged by most authorities not only as authentically by Paul, but also as his earliest extant letter, composed around AD 50. It begins in exactly the same way as its imitator, 2 Thessalonians, that is, with Paul acknowledging that he has two coauthors, Silvanus and Timothy.

Thessalonica was the capital of Macedonia, and Paul established his colony of Christians there on his second missionary journey. In the letter, he recalls their conversion "from idols to a living and true God" (1 Thess 1:9), but he also says that he faced great opposition when he was there (2:2). He goes on to characterize God Himself as "a tester of hearts" (2:4). Then Paul says that, after he departed from them, he wished, again and again, to return to them, "but Satan blocked our way" (2:18). (By the way, Paul

36

always refers to Satan as "Satan"—that is, *ho satanas*, based on Aramaic *Satanah*—never as "Devil.")

We remember that the earliest non-human satan in the Old Testament was played by the Angel of the Lord, who blocked the road of Balaam on his way to the Moabites. But that intervention was for a good purpose, and surely it should not be compared to Satan's interference with Paul's divinely sanctioned mission here? Well, maybe or maybe not. But in any case it could be construed as a test/temptation, one that was intended to "try men's souls," in the same way that God does.

We find a confirmation of the latter kind of thinking soon after, when Paul says that he was worried about how the Thessalonians were holding to the faith, so he sent Timothy to find out (here he speaks of his coauthor in the third person). "I was afraid," Paul says, "that somehow the tester (*ho peirazōn*) had tested you," and, he implies, that they had failed the test—"and that our labor had been in vain" (1 Thess 3:5). But Timothy returned with the good news of their faith and love.

So, does Paul think that his fears were unfounded? That "Satan the tester" had not tested them after all? Or does he believe that he did test them and that they passed the test (resisted the temptation)? We do not know, but he goes on in an apocalyptic mode in the last two chapters, warning his readers to be ready for the end, when the Lord will come again. First, he says he will come at the archangel's call and the sound of God's trumpet (1 Thess 4:16), but then he says that he will come like a thief in the night (1 Thess 5:3). His final advice to them is that they themselves are to become testers in a different sense: they are to test everything, to judge whether or not each action is the right thing to do (1 Thess 5:21–22).

In Paul's next earliest surviving letter, the First Epistle to the Corinthians, written a few years after the one he sent to the Thessalonians, he names Sosthenes as a coauthor. In it, he takes up some of the problems in Corinth that had been reported to him in his absence.

He is particularly shocked by one situation that was described to him; it will reveal ideas that he has about Satan that are completely unprecedented, as far as I know. The facts were these: one of the members of the church there had taken up living with a woman who had been his father's wife or concubine or mistress, and his fellow Christians did not rebuke him. Paul is outraged, and insists that the culprit is to be expelled from the community. He tells them, "You are to hand this man over to Satan for the destruction of the flesh, so that his spirit may be saved in the day of the Lord" (1 Cor 5:5).

What does he mean? He must see Satan as somehow having a punitive function, but one that not only punishes but also rehabilitates. We will see a similar idea in one of the Deutero-Pauline epistles, 1 Timothy. Nowadays, we might think of an enlightened warden of a penitentiary, with programs of remedial education aimed at making the inmates productive members of society when their time of incarceration is over.

It may be that Paul considers Satan to be "the ruler of the world," as we will find in the Gospels of Luke and John, and that the secular authorities that prosecute and punish criminal offenders come under his jurisdiction. Usually "the day of the Lord" is taken to mean the Last Judgment on the return of Jesus, but even if that is Paul's meaning here, it would not preclude the sense that the sinner is to be reformed in his lifetime.

The important point for us to underline in this passage is that both of Satan's functions here, punishing and reforming, are beneficial: he is a do-gooder.

A bit later in the epistle, Paul reminds the Corinthians that "we will judge angels" (1 Cor 6:3), seemingly again referring to the Last Judgment. Perhaps one of the angels to be judged will be Satan, on matters of dereliction of duty or malfeasance, which may or may not be "capital" offenses. One takeaway point is that, if Satan is in charge of secular justice, then he must be held responsible for all miscarriages of justice, which might entail dismissal from office, if not some disciplinary action against him, temporary or permanent.

38

When Satan appears again in the epistle, it is in the more expected context of testing, as Paul takes up the question of whether the single life is to be preferred to marriage. A further question arises within marriage: should spouses abstain from intercourse, out of devotion or asceticism? Paul's answer is that abstinence is certainly never mandatory, but it might be a worthy practice to hold off marital embraces for a period, in order to have more time for undistracted prayer. But the abstinence should not be too prolonged, "for fear that Satan might put you to the test and you lose control of yourselves" (1 Cor 7:5). In other words, we should not push ourselves beyond our limits, even for admirable motives, because it could provide an opportunity for Satan to prove that our virtue and self-control are a sham.

Satan is seen here in his more usual occupation of prodding humans to expose their underlying true nature. It would be natural if Satan had the reputation of finding more satisfaction in uncovering vice than in finding steadfastness in the persons he tests. We can infer even in the book of Job that Devil/Satan was disappointed that Job did not "curse the Lord to His face," as he predicted that he would.

The idea of testing comes up again later in 1 Corinthians, first when Paul reminds his listeners of what happened when the Jews in the desert tested God—they were punished by an infestation of poisonous serpents, and those who complained were cut down by the destroying angel (1 Cor 10:5–10)—the sort of punishing action that Paul might naturally think would lie in Satan's bailiwick. Remember that Paul told the Thessalonians that they were to test all things, but of course he did not mean that they should test God; it is meant to work the other way round!

Paul says that the experiences of the Jews in the desert are meant to serve as an example to us. We must always be on guard against succumbing to tests. Tests (that is, temptations) are common to everyone and constant, and we must constantly be on guard against them. However, he adds, "God is faithful, and will not let you be tested beyond your strength. For along with the tests He will also provide the means to remain steadfast, so that you may always be able to endure them" (1 Cor 10:13). In other words, even when Satan is directly involved in the testing, God makes sure that he does not overdo it. If the human objects of his attention fail the test, it is their own fault.

Chapter 11

Paul's Satan as challenger, and guardian against pride: 2 Corinthians

In Paul's Second Letter to the Corinthians (where Timothy joins him again as coauthor), Paul himself emerges as a satan, a testing adversary, since he admits that he devised a test for them to see if they would remain steadfast in their beliefs and actions. He says, "I wrote," in a letter that has not survived, "for this reason: to test you and to know whether you are obedient in everything" (2 Cor 2:4–9).

He says that he wrote in much anguish, though not with the intention to cause them pain, but to show them the great love that he had for them. The letter concerned a member of their congregation who had committed some offense, and who had been expelled from their fellowship, much in the way that Paul had insisted should be done with the sexual offender of 1 Corinthians. In fact, the traditional interpretation of this passage in 2 Corinthians is that it refers to the same person that Paul spoke of in 1 Corinthians; in other words, the sinner had completed his punishment and rehabilitation under Satan, and now had rejoined the community.

In any case, it shows that a person could be expelled and readmitted. That, in fact, was the test that Paul was submitting the Corinthians to; he wanted them to forgive and console the reformed offender so that he would not feel excessive distress. Apparently, they passed the test and complied with Paul's wishes. Paul adds, cryptically, that he forgives everyone whom they forgive, and everything that he has forgiven has been for their sake, "in order that we not be outwitted by Satan, for we are well aware of his machinations" (2 Cor 2:11).

We seem to have here an effort on Paul's part to circumvent a test devised by Satan by devising a test of his own. May the best tester win! He obviously thinks that he has succeeded. He was hoping for the best in his testing, whereas obviously Satan was hoping for the worst. This is what Paul means when he says that he is well aware of Satan's intentions.

Paul speaks of a further testing of the Corinthians when he asks them to contribute to the support of other Christian communities. "I do not command this, but I am testing the sincerity of your love against the generosity of others" (2 Cor 8:8). He challenges them to make responses similar to those of other churches: "Through the testing of this ministration, you glorify God, confessing the Gospel of Christ by your generosity" (2 Cor 9:13).

Many readers of Paul's letter have seen a further reference to Satan's tactics when he speaks of his success and lack of success in preaching the Gospel, saying that, for some persons, a veil or barrier has been set up to prevent the message from getting through. This has happened, he says, only in the case of those who are already perishing. He points to the one who is responsible for the maneuver: "The god of this age has blinded the minds of the unbelievers, to keep them from seeing the light of the gospel of the glory of Christ, who is the image of God" (2 Cor 4:3–4). That is the way it is usually translated, and "the god of this age" is usually taken to be Satan. If true, it would indicate Paul's belief that Satan had been put in charge of ruling the world—a belief that we will see explicitly stated elsewhere in the New Testament. Paul's idea in his earlier letter to the Corinthians—that Satan was the punisher and rehabilitator of the man who took up with his stepmother— would be a confirmation of this belief.

But the Greek phrase in question, *ho theos tou aiōnis toutou,* could be translated as "God at this time," and refer to Yahweh's dealings in the Old Testament with those who are unreceptive to His commands by making them even more unreceptive. The Lord tells Isaiah, "Make this people's heart coarse, make their ears dull, shut their eyes tight" (Isa 6:10). We can readily see God doing the same here—or commanding Satan to do it. It amounts to the same thing, after all, since Satan's activities are under God's supervision, and, as we heard Paul say, God will never let it get out of control beyond the powers of human resistance.

Paul definitely refers to Satan's stratagems further on in 2 Corinthians, when he explicitly describes the hypocritical approaches of rival Christian preachers: "They are pseudo-apostles, deceitful workers, transforming themselves into apostles of Christ." It is no wonder that they do this, he adds, "for Satan himself transforms himself into an angel of light" (2 Cor 11:13–14)—or perhaps he means "a shining angel" or only "a messenger of truth." He continues in the next verse: "So it is not strange if Satan's servants ['deacons'] also disguise themselves as ministers of uprightness. They will end up according to their deeds" (2 Cor 11:15).

We can only guess how Paul conceives of Satan here. He is seemingly contrasting him with celestial messengers, perhaps in the numerous instances in which "the angel of the Lord" appeared to the prophets of old. Earlier, Paul appeared to compare himself as a truthful minister of Christ to an angel coming out from the presence of God: "as from God, standing before God, speaking in Christ" (2 Cor 2:17).

An even more interesting reference appears later, when Paul speaks of "an angel of Satan," where Satan is clearly working in tandem with God for Paul's own betterment. Paul has felt obliged to boast of the spiritual favors he has received from God, but then he explains that a mechanism was put in place to prevent him from taking excessive pride in his accomplishments:

> To keep me from rising above myself, I was given a thorn in my flesh, an angel of Satan, to strike at me, to keep me from being puffed up. Three times I have pleaded with the Lord about this, to take it away from me, but He said to me, "My grace is enough for you, to let my power to show through your weakness." Therefore I will boast of

43

my weaknesses most of all, so that the power of Christ
may show forth in me. (2 Cor 12:7–9)

The thorn in the flesh that constituted the angel or messenger of
Satan has been variously explained, from a physical illness to an
obnoxious opponent or even colleague.

But whatever it was, Paul was sufficiently disturbed by it to
want to be rid of it with all his heart. And from the response that
he received from the Lord we can understand that Paul was being
tempted to react in some inappropriate or sinful way: a veritable
temptation of Satan. And yet, the purpose of the burdensome
thorn was entirely good, to prevent him from another kind of sin,
pride.

This is the clearest indication so far that Satan's activities can
be seen as no different from those manifested in the book of Job,
where he operated on consultation with God—although with a
certain amount of freedom. He was instructed there, "All that Job
has I put into your power, but do not touch his body" (Job 1:2),
and "I am giving him up to you, but you must spare his life" (2:6).
Just as we can easily infer that Satan is disappointed that his prediction that Job would crumble under the assaults did not come
true, we are doubtless justified in imagining the same thing about
the trial he imposes on Paul.

Paul ends the letter by returning to the theme of testing. The
Corinthians will test Paul to see if he speaks with the words of
Christ and carries through on his promise to treat sinners severely.
He responds by telling them to test themselves on their faith in
Christ, and not to fail it, whether he himself seems to pass their
test or not; the important thing is that they abstain from wrongdo-
ing (2 Cor 13:1–7). In the midst of all this talk of mutual testing at
the close of his letter, Satan has been forgotten.

Chapter 12

Paul on Adam: no Satan; Satan returns as roadblock (Romans 16)

Second Corinthians is the most Satan-filled of Paul's epistles, but most readers have found even more satanic references than I do. They assume, for instance, that when Paul asks, "What agreement does Christ have with Beliar?" (2 Cor 6:15), that Beliar is Satan. But there is no justification for this identification. Beliar or Belial in the Old Testament is a mere abstraction, standing for the total loss that comes with death, and there is no reason to think that Paul means anything else by Beliar here. I noted earlier that the lifeless figure of Belial in the Dead Sea Scrolls is similar. Likewise, as we will soon see, there is no justification for assuming that when Paul speaks of the Eden serpent he means Satan (2 Cor 11:3).

There are no specific references to Satan in Paul's other genuine letters, the relatively short messages to the Galatians and to the Philippians, or in his longest letter, Romans, except in a coda to the main text (Rom 16:20), which is likewise connected by almost all modern readers with the Eden serpent.

First we must deal with Paul's take on the Adam story, and for that we have to catch up with the Adam story itself. We saw in chapter 7 above that it was a late addition to Genesis, and when it began to be noticed, it was mainly in positive terms. The earliest such reference is in the book of Tobit, around 200 BC, where Tobias prays to God: "You made Adam and gave to him his wife Eve as a helper and support, and from them came the race of humankind.

You said, 'It is not good for the man to remain alone; let us make a helper for him like himself'" (Tob 8:6, citing Gen 2:18). The only reference Jesus makes to the Adam story in the Gospels is similar: he speaks of Eve's creation from Adam's rib, and the command of leaving father and mother and becoming two in one flesh (Mark 10:6–8; Matt 19:4–5).

Next is in Ben Sira, originally composed in Hebrew before ~180 BC, where the first man is treated very favorably, including a specific reference to Adam: "Shem and Seth and Enosh were honored, but beyond every other created living being was Adam" (Sir 49:16).

The widely read *Book of Enoch*, produced about the same time as Ben Sira was writing, which is cited in the New Testament for its story of the angels who mated with women (Jude 6; 2 Pet 2:4), deals lightly with the sin of Adam and Eve without mentioning the serpent. Raphael tells Enoch: "This is the Tree of Knowledge, from which your father of old and your mother of old did eat, and they learned knowledge, and their eyes were opened, and they understood that they were naked, and they were driven out of the garden" (1 En 32:6). The slightly later *Book of Jubilees*, however, tells the story straightforwardly, including the role of the serpent and its punishment: the Lord cursed the serpent, and His anger against it would remain forever (Jub 3:23).

We have seen in chapter 8 that the book of Wisdom glosses over Adam's transgression as relatively minor, made good by Wisdom's direction, leaving him as an exemplar of a good man, in contrast to his wicked son, Cain.

In our review of the Genesis account of Adam and Eve, we saw that God's threat of death on the very day of eating the forbidden fruit was not carried out. *Jubilees*, however, claimed that it was, saying that God was speaking of the heavenly day that lasts a thousand years, and Adam died when only 930 years old (Jub 4:30). The Egyptian Jewish philosopher Philo, who lived not long before Paul, came up with the explanation that the threat referred not to physical life but to the life of virtue, which was extinguished in Adam and Eve by their sin (*Allegorical Interpretation of Genesis* 1:105–7).

Paul has an explanation similar to that of Philo, distinguishing between death of the body and moral or spiritual death, but he does not articulate it clearly. He says that death was the punishment not only for Adam but also for Adam's progeny: "As all die in Adam, so all will be made alive in Christ" (1 Cor 15:22), but it is evident that he is not speaking about physical death, which all humans continued to suffer even after Christ's redeeming actions. His meaning is expressed very densely in Romans (5:12–21). Unlike Philo, who took the punitive death to be a descent into vice, which was reversible, Paul's metaphorical death was a condemnation that humans could not reverse on their own.

For Philo, the serpent was simply an animal, at once the cleverest and basest, which at the beginning had the power of speech; but allegorically it represented passion and desire (*Questions and Answers on Genesis* 31–32, 36, 47). There is no reason to believe that Paul thought of it any differently from how it is described in Genesis: "The serpent was the most sagacious of all the wild animals which the Lord God had made upon the earth" (Gen 3:1).

Paul refers to the Eden serpent only once, when he tells the Corinthians, "Just as the serpent with his cunning deceived Eve, so too you may be led astray from pure devotion to Christ" (2 Cor 11:3). The serpent's cunning is being compared to the distorted message of the "super-apostles."

The deception of Eve is mentioned only one other time in the New Testament, namely, in a letter written by one of Paul's disciples in Paul's name, as if Paul were actually the author. This Pseudo-Paul pretends to be writing to Timothy, Paul's sometime coauthor, and he gives him advice on how to keep women in their place:

> Women should take instruction and learn in all submission. I permit no woman to teach or to exercise the authority of a man; they are to remain silent. It was Adam who was formed first, and then Eve. It was not Adam who was deceived into transgressing, but the woman.

> But women will be saved through childbearing, if they
> live a faithful life with love, holiness, and modesty.
> (1 Tim 2:11–15)

We note that Pseudo-Paul does not even mention the serpent. As we shall see below, however, he does speak significantly of Satan, but not in connection with the first parents.

Now let us look at Paul's sign-off reference to Satan in Romans, in the midst of various postscripts, including another warning against false teachers. Then comes either a prayer or a prophecy, depending on the textual variant chosen: "May the God of peace soon crush Satan beneath your feet," or "The God of peace will soon crush Satan beneath your feet" (Rom 16:20).

As noted, readers have typically taken Paul's words to refer to the punishment of the Eden serpent, and therefore have assumed that he is identifying Satan with the serpent. Aside from the fact that any such identification is completely unwarranted at this early date, in the first century AD, the language of the passage does not support it. Paul almost always cites the Septuagint version of the Old Testament rather than the Hebrew text, and there the sentence on the serpent reads, "I will put enmity between you and the woman, and between your offspring and hers: he will watch against your head, and you will watch against his heel" (LXX Gen 3:15). The Hebrew text for the last part has instead, "he will strike at your head, and you will strike at his heel." It is quite clear in both versions that an ongoing sparring is intended, not an ultimate elimination of all serpents. The idea of a crushing victory over the serpent's offspring is an over-reading fueled by later typological fantasies, taking the passage as a prediction of Mary's son Jesus defeating Satan.

When we clear away such elaborations and look with cool eyes at the text of Romans, in the light of other things that Paul has said about Satan, an obvious interpretation is that the Apostle is regarding him in his obstructionist role; he is a roadblock interfering with the progress of the Christian community, and God will see to it, Paul prays or predicts, by demolishing the obstruction. Later on, in Matthew's Gospel, we will see Jesus not only naming

48

Peter Satan for arguing against his return to Jerusalem, but also calling him a stumbling block (*skandalon*) (Matt 16:23).

We can sum up Paul's assessments of Satan by saying that he sees him as a personage with authority not only over spiritual testing but also over secular government, policing, punishing, and correcting. He impedes and tempts to discouragement (1 Thessalonians), he convicts and punishes but also rehabilitates sinners, after having tempted them to commit misdeeds in the first place (1 Corinthians). One must be aware of his stratagems and deceptive enticements as an angel of light, even when ostensibly acting to prevent sin, like Paul's becoming proud of the favors he has received (2 Corinthians). But Paul hopes and prays that God will soon restrain his activities (Rom 16). In his other genuine epistles, namely, Philippians and Galatians and the brief note to Philemon, he makes no allusion to Satan, even though there was seemingly much opportunity to do so, because he often speaks of opponents to the true faith that he preaches. No matter who it is that proclaims doctrine different from what he has taught, even an angel from heaven, he should be condemned (Gal 1:8). If any among the Galatians has trespassed, he is to be restored in a spirit of meekness, and each is to take care not to be tempted (Gal 6:1). Paul urges the faithful at Philippi not to be intimidated by their opponents (Phil 1:27–28). Some enemies are dogs who tear the flesh (Phil 3:2), and others oppose the cross of Christ, their god is their belly, their minds set on earthly things (Phil 3:18–19). One might assume that Satan was behind them, but the possibility is passed over in silence. *An exaggeration.*

PART 4

The Gospels

Chapter 13

Mark's Satan: testing Jesus

Mark's Gospel is the shortest and earliest of the four Gospels. By the way, we often hear of other gospels, usually called "apocryphal," like the *Gospel of Thomas* or the *Gospel of Judas*. But these are modern titles. The fact is, the title "Gospel" (Greek *euangelion*) in the ancient world is used only for the four writings called such in the New Testament.

Mark's work is called "The Gospel of Jesus Christ," but it starts not with Jesus but with John the Baptist, who predicts a mightier preacher than himself. When Jesus comes and is baptized by John, the Spirit like a dove comes down upon him, and a voice is heard saying, "You are my beloved son: with you I am well pleased" (Mark 1:11).

Surely this ringing endorsement from God Himself would be sufficient for Satan, and he would concede that Jesus needed no testing. But perhaps the ruling paradigm here is the scene at the opening of the book of Job, where God expresses great satisfaction with Job, only to be challenged by Satan, that he needs to be tried before he can be pronounced true.

Let us see what happens here: "And immediately the Spirit sends him out into the desert, and he remained in the desert for forty days, where he was tested by Satan, in the midst of wild animals, and he was ministered to by angels" (Mark 1:12–13). It is not at Satan's petition that Jesus is tested, but at the initiative of the Spirit that descended upon him from the heavens. The forty days of trial in the desert were undoubtedly meant to call up the forty years' sojourn of the Israelites in the wilderness under Moses's lead.

In the story of Job, the testing angel, Satan, stayed in the background, but in the story of Balaam, the "satanic angel" actually appeared to the prophet, and in the story of Joshua the high priest in Zechariah, two angels, Satan and the Angel of Yahweh, disputed over him after he had obviously failed in whatever tests he had been put to, which had made him guilty and his garments filthy.

In Mark, Jesus is said to be not only with animals but also with angels, who served. The usual assumption is that they served him only after Satan's departure, which is the way Matthew will stage the scene. But Mark may have intended the angelic assistance to take place during his trials. At the end, Mark does not bother to state the obvious conclusion, that Jesus withstood Satan's tests superlatively.

Apart from Job, the main figure to test well in the Old Testament was Abraham, and a tradition of his many tests was built up from what was read in Genesis 22:1: "After these things God tested Abraham," understood to mean, "After these tests God tested Abraham yet again" with the most severe trial of all, by ordering him to kill his son Isaac as a sacrifice. A Jewish work called the *Apocalypse of Abraham*, dating from the late first century AD, elaborates a trial of Abraham from an earlier episode in Genesis, where God orders him to make animal sacrifices (Gen 15:9–13). The author rewrites the story to take place after a forty-day fast. Abraham is assisted by a protective angel, Jaoel, but another angel, Azazel (who had a bad reputation as the leader of the angels who mated with women in the *Book of Enoch*), tries to persuade him not to proceed, to no avail. Perhaps Mark was drawing on a similar tradition.

Much of what follows in Mark's Gospel centers upon Jesus's activity in healing diseases, including some seemingly endemic to the Galilean countryside, caused by invisible parasites called "demonians" or demons, or filthy spirits, which differ from our modern bacteria and viruses by possessing knowledge and an ability to speak. They know that Jesus is a holy person, and fear that he has come to destroy them.

The demons have no obvious connection with Satan, but some sort of connection is made later, when a group of scribes, that is, legal experts, from Jerusalem mock Jesus and his supposed ability to expel these talking parasites. Judeans seem to have been skeptical of the existence of the demons that Galileans thought they were afflicted with. Presumably, they would have diagnosed a supposed demonic voice coming out of a person as simply the person's own voice, just as we would today.

The scribes say that Jesus can expel demons from other people because he himself is possessed by the chief demon, whose name is Beelzebul: "He has Beelzebul, so it's by the ruler of demons that he drives out demons" (Mark 3:22). Jesus pretends to take them seriously, and says that what they assert makes no sense: why would the head demon act against other demons? As Mark says, "he spoke to them in comparisons"—which is what *parabola* means. The first comparison he gives is, "How can a satan drive out a satan?" We can tell that he is using the common word "satan" here, because there is no definite article. He is saying, in effect, "That would be like one adversary throwing out a fellow adversary." The second comparison is, "If a kingdom is divided against itself, it cannot last," and the third is like it: "If a household is at odds with itself, it cannot hold together." It is the fourth comparison that most concerns us: "If Satan were to fight against himself, he could not carry on—he would be finished." Or, more literally: "If Satan has risen up against himself and is divided, he cannot stand, but his end has come." The last comparison is not so obvious: if you are a robber and want to rob a house owned by a strong man, you must first subdue the owner (Mark 3:23–28).

Because readers of this passage have not recognized that Jesus is giving several unconnected examples, they have assumed, since he mentions Satan in one of them (or, they think, in two of them), that the whole passage deals with Satan. Therefore, in the light of many other facts supposedly known about Satan, various conclusions have been drawn from these verses, including the following:

1. Satan is the chief demon.

2. Beelzebul is another name for Satan.

3. Demons are satans or devils of the same nature as Satan, that is, fallen angels.

4. Like his fellow devils, Satan himself possesses people, and it would make no sense for him to eject himself from one of his victims.

5. Satan has a united and highly successful organization.

6. There is no way that Satan would act against himself or perform any action contrary to his evil goals.

7. The only way to dismantle Satan's kingdom is to defeat its strong leader, namely, Satan himself, and that is what Jesus will do by dying on the cross.

Now, however, if we concede that Jesus brings up Satan only in the fourth comparison, what exactly is he saying about him? The only information that Mark has given us before this about Satan was in the first chapter; he says that he tested Jesus for forty days in the desert. Here, in chapter 3, he says that it would be unthinkable for Satan to rise up against himself; otherwise, he would not still be able to function. But, since he is clearly still functioning, the end of his position or appointment (whatever that is) is nowhere in sight.

In chapter 4, Mark brings up Satan after telling the long comparison or parable about the sower and his seeds. Jesus admits that his parables are intended to mystify unsympathetic listeners to his discourses "so that when they look they do not really see, and when they hear they do not really take it in" (Mark 4:12), referring to God's command to Isaiah cited in chapter 11 above: "Make this people's heart coarse, make their ears dull, shut their eyes tight" (Isa 6:10).

The real meaning of this parable, he tells his disciples, is this: The word of God comes not only to persons who are deaf because of their own fault. In addition there is a personage who deliberately keeps the message from being absorbed, namely Satan, for,

56

"as soon as some people hear the word, Satan comes and takes it away from them" (Mark 4:15).

Satan is clearly exercising his obstructionist or impeding functions here, but he can be thought of as simply complementing the sort of miscommunication that Jesus himself was practicing, like Isaiah, as ordered by God, towards people who through their own fault or failing were not ready to hear the truth.

Satan makes no further appearance in Mark's Gospel, except at the point where Peter attempts to persuade Jesus not to go to Jerusalem to his death. Jesus sharply rebukes him, calling him Satan, and telling him to get out of the way: "Get behind me, Satan! Your concerns are not God's but men's!" (Mark 8:33). Needless to say, Jesus is also asserting that they are not only human concerns, but also the concerns of Satan to test Jesus once again by trying to keep him from fulfilling his mission and destiny.

That in fact would seem to sum up Mark's view of Satan: his "standing orders," so to speak, were to put people through their paces by enticing them to deviate from their duty to God. Towards the end of his Gospel, when Jesus is praying in the Garden of Olives, he comes to his slumbering apostles and tells Peter to wake up and pray against the time of testing: no matter how strong his spirit is, his flesh is weak (Mark 14:38). Jesus does not say that it will be Satan who will do the testing, but it is a good bet.

Chapter 14

Matthew's Satan: trading Scripture with Jesus

In this chapter, we will examine the ways in which Matthew added
to what Mark says about Satan. The most striking thing comes at
the beginning, in elaborating the trials that Satan subjected Jesus
to in the desert. Rather than seeing him tested for forty days, we
find here only that Jesus fasted for forty days (Matt 4:2), like Moses
before receiving the tablets of the Law (Deut 9:9). But at the end
of this time, Jesus did not receive a communication from God, like
Moses, but rather a series of suggestions from Satan.

This presentation, adopted also by Luke, thought by many
scholars to be from an intermediate Gospel they call "Q," is the
most extraordinary episode in all the Gospels. It was clearly not
meant to be taken as a real event. Rather it is a kind of dramatic
elaboration on events, of the sort that Hebrew biblical commentators would call a midrash. It is also like the fictional parables that
Jesus tells to make his points.

So, Mark's simple statement is transformed into a set of encounters with Satan, the tester-in-chief. Satan actually meets with
Jesus as if he were a fellow rabbi presenting a series of challenges,
to which Jesus replies with the correct answers, all taken from the
Torah. Satan not only speaks with Jesus, he "takes" him instantly
to the top of the Temple, and then flies him to an impossibly high
mountain.

We can speculate that the Q gospel author was inspired by the
words of God spoken after Jesus was baptized: "This is my beloved

58

son, in whom I am well pleased" (Matt 3:17); he would have seen the resemblance to God's praise of Job when speaking to Satan, as "a man more than all men blameless, true, devout, and avoiding every bad deed" (Job 1:8). Satan made it his business to prove God wrong then, and he will try to do the same now. Just as Satan saw this as a challenge to overcome Job's virtue, so here Satan would subject Jesus to tests to uncover his shortcomings or to lead him astray from his proper course of action.

But instead of the kind of disaster-testing resorted to by Satan against Job, Q decided to parallel the tests that God Himself inflicted on the Israelites in the desert. No doubt he took his cue from Deuteronomy 8:2: "You shall remember all of the ways in which the Lord your God led you about in the desert, afflicting you and testing you in order to know your heart, to see if you will obey His commands." As we will see, Jesus's response to the first test draws on the very next verse: "And He afflicted you and starved you, and then fed you with manna, which was unknown to your fathers, to teach you that man shall not live on bread alone, but on every word that comes from God's mouth" (Deut 8:3).

Here is the first act of Q's temptation drama:

> Then Jesus was led up into the desert by the Spirit to be tested by Devil. And having fasted for forty days and forty nights, he was hungry.
>
> Then the tester approached him and said, "If you are a son of God, tell these stones to become loaves of bread."
>
> But he answered and said, "It is written, 'Man does not live on bread alone, but on every word that comes from God's mouth.'" (Matt 4:1–4)

The purport of this lesson is not readily understandable, whether in the original context of Deuteronomy or in its present application. Traditionally, it has been taken to mean that rather than use his powers for himself, Jesus will await God's will. Or it may simply mean that spiritual nourishment is more important than physical sustenance. Bread and testing, and perhaps Satan, will be collocated later on in Matthew, in the Lord's Prayer.

We notice that Q seemingly portrays Satan and Jesus as well acquainted with each other. This becomes clearer in the second tableau, which requires Jesus's full cooperation in "going along with Satan":

> Then Devil took him into the Holy City and set him on a pinnacle of the Temple, and said to him, "If you are a son of God, throw yourself down. For it is written, 'He will command His angels on your behalf,' and 'they will take hold of you in their hands, to keep your feet from hitting the stones below.'"
>
> Jesus answered, "Another Scripture says, 'You shall not test the Lord your God.'" (Matt 4:5–7)

Satan quotes here verses from Psalm 90 (91), *Qui habitat*, beginning, "Whoever dwells in the help of the Most High will be sheltered by the God of heaven." The hyper-optimistic verses of the psalm were taken to refer to a messianic figure, a very special "son of God." Jesus resists Satan's temptation to take the words of the psalm as meant for him. He recalls Moses's words to the Israelites, "You shall not test the Lord thy God, as you tested Him in the Place of Testing" (Deut 6:16). This refers to the time that the wandering Israelites were lacking not food but water, and they began to complain against Moses for bringing them out of Egypt to die of thirst. Moses considered such complaining to be the equivalent of testing God. After producing water miraculously by striking a rock with his staff, he called the locale the Place of Testing, where the people tested the Lord. Their testing consisted of asking, "Is the Lord here or not?" (Exod 17:1–7). That is, they challenged God to prove that He had concern for them and would help them in their extremity.

Jesus, of course, was in no further extremity than his hunger. But Satan was inviting him to invent an extremity to see if God would rescue him; and Jesus, naturally, showed his rectitude by declining the invitation.

The third test follows:

> Next, Devil took him to a very high mountain and showed him all the kingdoms of the world in all their

glory. He said to him, "I will give you all this if you will bow down and show me homage."

Then Jesus said to him, "Go away, Satan. For it is written, 'You shall do homage to the Lord your God, and serve only Him.'"

Then Devil left him, and suddenly angels appeared and ministered to him. (Matt 4:8–11)

Jesus's citation is of Deuteronomy 6:13, with the Septuagint variant of "do homage to" rather than "fear" the Lord. The command comes after Moses says that the Lord will supply all sorts of worldly benefits to Israelites, and it is followed by a warning not to follow after the gods of other nations.

Satan's test has been interpreted as involving a claim on his part to be a rival of God and as offering material goods and power in exchange for transferring his allegiance away from God to Satan. But such a reading is too much influenced by post-biblical notions of Satan as an enemy of God. If we recognize him instead as God's agent with a particular portfolio, our perspective changes. Satan should be seen instead as offering to incorporate Jesus into his own mission of policing the world. This interpretation will become clearer in Luke's presentation.

All three tests should be taken not only as reflecting the testing of the Israelites in the desert, but also as testing the messianic role of Jesus, by inviting him to assume the sort of physically aggressive goals of a military messiah, goals that would exalt his own standing and seek to overthrow Roman power.

The three-part testing of Jesus in the desert might have been partially inspired by Mark's portrayal of Peter being challenged three times to admit to being a follower of Jesus (Mark 14:66–72, taken over by Matt 26:69–75). It also parallels Mark's earlier presentation of Jesus's threefold petition to God to be relieved of his duty, where, as we saw, he also warns Peter to be wary of testing, that is, of "entering into temptation" (Mark 14:32–42, Matt 26:36–46). We have also seen Paul's threefold petition to be delivered from the angel of Satan that was tormenting him (2 Cor 12:70–79).

At the point where Matthew takes over Mark's episode of Jesus calling Peter Satan (for trying to talk him out of fulfilling his mission of going to his death in Jerusalem), Matthew adds that Jesus also calls him a stumbling block, that is, a *skandalon*, who should stop obstructing him—a classic role of Satan (Matt 16:23).

Matthew presents Satan in the desert as claiming ownership of all of the kingdoms of the world. In taking over the Beelzebul episode from Mark, he reduces the number of mini-comparisons or parables from five to four by leaving out the first, about rival satans, but he expands the one dealing with Satan to suggest that he has a kingdom: "If Satan were to cast out Satan, he would be divided against himself. How then would his kingdom survive?" (Matt 12:26). Perhaps we are to think that his rule over all human kingdoms is regarded as a single gigantic monarchy.

Much later in his Gospel, Matthew tells of the end of the world, when Jesus will reward those who have brought aid to the suffering people and punish those who failed to do so; he will send the latter "to the fire of the next aeon prepared for Devil and his angels" (Matt 25:41). This is usually taken to mean that Devil and his ministers will be punished along with the human beings who have failed the all-important test of charity. But the true meaning may be that, just as Satan was in charge of policing the present world, so too he will supervise the punishment of wrongdoers in the afterlife. There is a similar treatment of Satan in the "book of Parables" added to the *Book of Enoch* around the time that the Christian Gospels were produced.

Chapter 15

Matthew's Satan as "evil"—or not so bad!

We have seen that Paul and Mark refer to Satan only as "Satan" (*ho Satanas*), and Matthew as both Satan and "Devil" (*ho Diabolos*). Matthew, like Paul (1 Thess 3:5), employs another designation, "the Testing One" (*ho peirazōn*).

Still another term appears in Matthew's next modification concerning Satan, *ho ponēros*, which is usually translated as "the Evil One." So, since he is evil, that would seem to end the discussion about his nature and function. He could hardly be working for God, could he? Surely, he must have undergone some radical transformation, like rebelling against God and becoming His enemy. Otherwise, how could the good God continue to employ him?

The problem, I respond, lies not so much in the nature and character of Satan as in the English word "evil," which, as applied to Satan, immediately summons up the quintessence of perversity, immorality, and utterly unredeemable depravity, what philosophers call "radical evil." Other languages are not so fortunate as to have a special word for "really bad," as opposed to "simply bad." For instance, Latin uses the same word, *malum*, and so does Italian (*malo*) and French (*mal*) and German (*böse*), all of them meaning the whole range from deeply malicious to merely naughty or unpleasant. We in English can speak of an evil genius but hardly an evil child or evil pet ("Evil dog! Evil dog!") or evil rainstorm. Admittedly, though, when we speak of the "problem of evil," we usually mean diseases and natural disasters rather than crimes committed by humans (or by Satan!).

By delivering ourselves from "evil" and using only "bad" and other equivalents, let us try to determine the most appropriate meanings to attach to *ponēros* when applied to Satan, that is, in light of the history of Satan seen so far (as opposed to what Satan will become in future centuries). Classically, *ponēros* can refer to things that are "toilsome," "painful," or "grievous." It can describe "a sorry state," "a bad case," "a terrible plight." People with this adjective applied to them can be "worthless" or "knavish," or "useless" or "good for nothing." It can be used for "sorry jests" or "a bad beginning." It is used for "bad words" (see Matt 5:11: "Blessed are you when they reproach you and persecute you and, lying, say all bad [*pan ponēron*] against you for my sake") or for "blemish" (see LXX Deuteronomy 17:1: "You shall not sacrifice to the Lord your God a calf or a sheep in which there is a defect or anything bad [*pan rhēma ponēron*]") or for "bad deeds" (see the next verses in Deuteronomy, 17:2–7, referring to "that which is bad" [*to ponēron*] and worthy of stoning). In a political sense, *ponēros* designates "those of the baser sort," in Latin, the *viles*, or "vile populace."

The Septuagint Deuteronomy uses the term to refer to "a bad sore" ("May the Lord smite you with an evil ulcer [*helkon ponēron*] on your knees and legs" [Deut 28:35]), and the same term is applied to the filthy spirits of the Synoptic Gospels, who, as we saw in the chapter on Mark, are only "bad" in a physical, not moral, sense—that is, they bear no ill will towards their hosts, and do not wish to make them sin, but only wish to have a good place to live. Satan, on the other hand, was perceived as having ill will and attempting to make persons sin, even though it might be for what he considered a good cause: to expose their inherent unworthiness to be counted among the blessed of God. So, in his case, appropriate translations of *ponēros* might be "ill-disposed," "harmful," "trouble-making," and even "malicious," or "malevolent," as long as it is understood that his malevolence is aimed at humankind and not at God—someone, in fact, like Shakespeare's Malvolio, a harsh and puritanical supervisor, feared and resented by his underlings. So, with this proviso, we can call him Malevolent.

In the parable of the Sower, then, where Mark said that it was Satan who took away the word, in Matthew it is Malevolent who prevents a certain sector of humanity from receiving the salutary message (Matt 13:19). Then Matthew has Jesus tell of another farmer who sowed his land with good seed, but an enemy of his came along that night and sowed weeds in the fields (Matt 13:24–30). Jesus later explains that the weeds stand for the sons of Malevolent, sowed by their father, Devil, who is the enemy of the story (Mt 13.38–39). "The Enemy" (*ho echthros*) will become another name for Satan. The weeds are later characterized as *skandalia*, stumbling blocks, which will be thrown into the fire and burned at the harvest at the end of time (Matt 13:41–42).

* * *

Matthew's version of the prayer that Jesus teaches to his disciples (6:9–13) goes beyond Luke's ending, "do not bring us into testing," and adds, "but keep us from malevolence"—or is it "from Malevolent"?

The Greek is in the genitive, *apo tou ponērou*, and we cannot tell whether it is abstract or personal, *to ponēron*, "malevolence," or personal, *ho ponēros*. If the latter, it could be proper or generic. If proper, it would undoubtedly refer to Satan, "the malevolent one." If generic, it would be "the malevolent person," meaning "any malevolent person," "all malevolent persons," "the malevolent."

Matthew provides examples of both personal usages in rapid succession in the previous chapter: "Say only 'Yes, yes' or 'No, no'; anything more comes from the Malevolent One (*apo tou ponērou*). You have heard it said, 'An eye for an eye, a tooth for a tooth'; but I say to you, offer no resistance to obnoxious persons (*tō ponērō*), but if one of them strikes you on the one cheek, turn the other to him" (Matt 5:37–39). So, in the first case, it probably means "Malevolent" (Satan), but it could mean "malevolence," or "malevolent person." In the second case, it obviously does not apply to Satan.

65

The King James Version takes it to mean "malevolence," rendering the clause, "that ye resist not evil." Most modern translations take it to refer to bad persons. Here are some examples:

NRSV   do not resist an evildoer

NJB   offer no resistance to the wicked

NAB   offer no resistance to one who is evil

REB   do not resist those who wrong you

NIV   do not resist an evil person

In light of all this, let us look at the Our Father and how it is or is not about Satan. Here is the text in Matthew (6:9–13):

> Our Father in heaven,
>
> May your name be revered;
>
> May your rule be manifest;
>
> May your will be performed here on earth just as it is in heaven.
>
> Give us today our daily bread.
>
> And forgive our debts, just as we have forgiven our own debtors.
>
> And do not draw us into testing,
>
> But deliver us from harm/Harm.

It is quite evident from the last two clauses that God Himself is involved in testing us. If the final word is impersonal, it means that God alone is seen as the tester, and the whole petition means, "We implore you to test us no more, but keep us from all danger"; or, "Keep us from succumbing to our present trials, and send us no more."

But if the last word refers to Satan, it means that God and Satan are involved together, as in the prime paradigm of the book of Job, and the petition must mean: "Do not authorize further testing for us, but refuse all of Satan's requests."

This would be a prayer similar to that of Paul in 2 Corinthians, in pleading three times to the Lord to remove the angel of Satan from him (2 Cor 12:7–9).

* * *

In summary we can say that Matthew's Satan sets himself the task
of "putting Jesus on trial in the field," thereby confronting him
with the goals and limits of his messianic role. He urges him to
use his powers for his own benefit, and to force God to intervene
to protect him from reckless adventures (testing God). He then
tries to co-opt Jesus to his own assignment of ruling the world,
thereby fulfilling the hopes of those awaiting a military messiah
(Matt 4:1–11). Satan's regimen is strong because of its unified
purpose (Matt 12:26), which is to assess the moral character of
human beings by various challenges that strike his victims as sheer
malevolence: he is the Malevolent One who fosters swearing (Matt
5:37), distorts the truth, and infiltrates the virtuous (Matt 13:19,
40). His new mission is to interfere as much as he can with Jesus's
mission, and Jesus sees Peter as doing Satan's work as a stumbling
block in trying to keep him from going to Jerusalem (Matt 16:23).
All of Satan's stumbling blocks will be burned at the final harvest
(Matt 13:42), and it may be Satan who does the burning (Matt
25:41). Jesus himself tells us to beg God to free us from the trials
that Satan seeks to impose on us (Matt 6:13).

Chapter 16

Luke's Satan: the appointed ruler of the world— due for a sudden fall

Luke's Gospel draws on Q as well as Mark, but rather than completely substituting Q's three-part drama for Mark's forty days of testing, Luke combines them: "Jesus was led about in the desert forty days, being tested by Devil" (Luke 4:1–2), and then he underwent the specific tests recounted in Matthew. However, the second and third tests are switched—the mountain view of the kingdoms of the world comes second, and the visit to the spire of the Temple comes third. Luke also makes an important addition to the kingdoms test. In offering Jesus all of the power and glory of the world, Satan says, "I will give it to you because it has been delivered to me, and I give it to whomever I wish" (Luke 4:6). That is to say, he here claims, without any contradiction from Jesus, that he has been appointed—obviously by God Himself—to rule over the world.

Satan offers to share this rule with Jesus, if he will only acknowledge his authority. As we concluded above in Matthew's presentation, it was Satan's suggestion that Jesus change the direction of his mission, whatever it is, and join Satan in his enterprises, which aim at taking people to task for their present character rather than changing them for the better. Paul's idea of Satan as rehabilitator does not make an appearance in the Gospels.

However, we have seen indications that Paul knew of the idea of Satan being in charge of secular justice, and we have speculated that it may have been seen as implied in the two celestial

68

appearances of Satan in the Old Testament, where, in the book of Job, he patrols the whole earth under heaven, and in Zechariah, he is the prosecutor of humans.

A parallel for God's delivery of the world over to Satan might be seen in the earlier prophet Jeremiah, in the revelation that Yahweh gave to him, that he was appointing His servant Nebuchadnezzar to rule over all of the people and animals of the earth, and his rule is to last, enforced by Yahweh Himself, until his time is up (Jer 27:5–8). In fact, in the Greek version of Jeremiah, God speaks in much the same way that Satan does in Luke: "I have made the earth and I will give it to whomever I please" (LXX Jer 34:5).

Luke also differs from the other two Synoptic evangelists in saying at the end of the temptation in the desert, "When Devil had finished every test, he departed from Jesus until an opportune time" (Luke 4:13). There is no explicit mention of Satan's return in the remainder of the Gospel, except when he co-opts Judas (Luke 22.3), but Jesus does make a prediction of Satan's coming fate, and he also tells of his activity against his apostles, as we will hear.

First, the prediction. It comes in chapter 10, at the point where Jesus has sent out a large group of his disciples to cure the sick and to announce the coming of the kingdom of Heaven. When the disciples return, jubilant over their success in healing demoniacs in the name of Jesus, Jesus responds by saying that Satan's reign would come to an end. He expresses it by saying that he could see it happening: "I was watching Satan fallen from the heavens, like a flash of lightning" (Luke 10:18).

Of course, many if not most readers of the Bible, relying on Miltonic images of a primordial rebellion and fall of Satan, assume that Jesus is speaking historically of a past rebellion and fall of Satan, and that, as Son of God, Jesus was actually on the scene in heaven when it happened. More sophisticated readers, well aware that Luke does not display any notion of the pre-existence of Jesus, conclude that he is speaking of a future cessation of Satan's authoritative position.

Some interpreters say that Satan's predicted loss of power is to come only at the end of the world, at the Last Judgment. It seems much more likely, however, that a sooner, if not immediate, downfall is intended. Jesus's remark is triggered by the disciples' enthusiastic reports on the inroads they have made against demons, and their progress in publicizing the coming kingdom of heaven.

Jesus goes on to tell them, "Behold, I have given you power to walk over serpents and scorpions and over all the force of the enemy, and nothing shall harm you. You should not rejoice because the spirits obey you, but rather because your names are written in the heavens" (Luke 10:19–20). The "enemy" undoubtedly refers to Satan, and Jesus says he has made the disciples immune to his power—surely an exaggeration, since they will always be liable to buckle under the assault of his trials. Or, he is assuming that they will overcome Satan if they use their resources properly, and do not take undue pride in them.

Therefore, we conclude that Jesus is asserting that Satan's powers are failing and that he is heading for a fall, like Nebuchadnezzar in Jeremiah's oracle, which will come with lightning speed and thunderous effect.

We see a different outlook for Satan in the Beelzebul episode of the next chapter. Luke, like Matthew, has Jesus refer to Satan's "kingdom," stressing that because Satan is not divided against himself, his reign is still strong (Luke 11:18).

Chapter 17

Luke on Satan's testing:
by disease-spirits and in person

Satan's connection with disease, whether caused by demons or not, is made most explicit in Luke's second book in the New Testament, the Acts of the Apostles, in the speech that Peter gives to the household of the centurion Cornelius, saying that Jesus "went about healing people who were afflicted by Devil" (Acts 10:38). But Luke also makes it clear in his Gospel, when he tells of the woman who approaches Jesus while he is teaching in the Temple. A "spirit" has crippled her for eighteen years, we are told, keeping her bent over all this time. When Jesus looks at her, she immediately straightens up at his words: "Woman, you are free of your infirmity" (Luke 13:11–13). Later, when he justifies healing her on the Sabbath, Jesus says that it was Satan who had held the woman in bondage for the eighteen years (Luke 13:16).

Luke has other interesting additions to the story of Satan later on in his Gospel, for instance, in chapter 22, right before Jesus's arrest and trials. He first speaks of the efforts of the chief priests and the scribes, just before the feast of Passover, to find a way of killing Jesus. Then, he says, "Satan entered into Judas Iscariot, one of the twelve, who went and plotted with the chief priests and the temple guard on how he could betray him. They received him eagerly, and agreed to give him silver" (Luke 22:3–4).

One likely interpretation of this statement is that Judas got wind of the conspiracy through the agency of Satan, and it

71

constituted a test for him, which he failed: he gave in to the prospect of earning money by facilitating their scheming. At the point at which he consented to go and deal with them, Luke says that Satan entered his heart.

Satan's action is not to be compared to the invasion of humans by the Galilean disease-demons that Luke and the other Synoptics (Mark and Matthew) speak of; this type of demon has nothing to do with temptation and sin, but only seeks bodies to inhabit, no matter how much it inconveniences or incapacitates its hosts. Rather, Satan's method with Judas is to be taken in that same way in which Luke in the Acts of the Apostles reports how Peter spoke to Ananias and Sapphira about their devious real-estate scheme. Peter is aware that they are attempting to deceive the apostles by pretending to give a generous gift to the community, whereas in reality they have surreptitiously kept part of the sale proceeds for themselves. He says to Ananias, "Why has Satan filled your heart, that you should deceive the Holy Spirit and keep part of the price?" His further question almost seems to question Satan's motive: "Why was this deed put into your heart? You have lied not to men but to the Holy Spirit." Further, he accuses them of putting God to the test (Acts 5:1–10). In other words, Satan tempted them to tempt God; they succumbed, and were struck dead, with no opportunity for repentance. Unlike Peter himself, they were not given a second chance.

Later on in Acts, Paul encounters opposition from a magician named Elymas bar-Jesus, that is, literally, "son of Jesus." Paul instead calls him "son of Devil" and "enemy of all goodness." But he fares better at Paul's hands than Ananias and Sapphira did at the hands of Peter, for Paul tells Elymas that the Lord will punish him by making him blind, but only "for a time" (Acts 13:6–11).

We must remember that Paul himself opposed the Christians, until he was struck blind; when his sight was restored, he became the greatest champion of the new movement (Acts 9:1–22). Luke has Paul himself recount this story twice (Acts 22:3–15 and 26:12–18). The second time, Paul says he heard Jesus tell him that he was sending him to open the eyes of the Gentiles, "so that they may

72

turn from darkness to light and from the power of Satan to God."
Calling Devil Satan sounds very Pauline, as does associating him
with darkness rather than light—though Satan can fake allegiance
by appearing as an "angel of light" (2 Cor 11:14).

Chapter 18

Luke's Satan in dialogue with God and Jesus

Luke's most interesting portrayal of Satan occurs at the Last Supper. Recall that after Satan tempted Jesus in the desert, Luke qualifies that Satan departed from him only until the time was again opportune (Luke 4:13), which invites the question, when did he return? He was certainly in the vicinity when he entered into Judas and pushed him to betray Jesus (Luke 22:3).

From what Jesus tells the apostles on their last evening together, it appears that Satan has been actively involved all along, and that Jesus was aware of it and undoubtedly knew about Satan's involvement in alienating Judas. Jesus reveals that one of the apostles will betray him (Luke 22:21). He then speaks of the other tests that he himself has already undergone, and which the apostles have shared and remained steadfast with him throughout. As a reward, they will sit on thrones and judge the twelve tribes of Israel (Luke 22:28–30).

Jesus then singles out Simon Peter and tells him, as the others listen, of a seeming encounter that he has had with both God and Satan. He says, "Simon, Simon, Satan has strongly demanded to sift all of you like wheat, and his request has been approved" (Luke 22:31). (All of this action is contained in the one Greek verb, *exētēsato*, meaning "he has successfully insisted.")

How does Jesus know this? He must have been present at the interview and intervened in the exchange, because he goes on to say: "But I made request concerning you," still addressing Simon

74

alone, "that your faith might not give way, so that, once you turn back again, you may support your brothers" (Luke 22:32).

In other words, just as Satan convinced God that Job needed more testing, so here Satan has urged that the tests the apostles had already successfully endured along with Jesus were not sufficient and that more trials of their fidelity are necessary. As in the case of Job, God agrees. Indeed, it was a foregone conclusion that their faith would fail, and that the temptations would be so extreme that they would give in. But then Jesus requested that Peter's fidelity would still be strong enough to recover and be sufficiently renewed to bring the others back as well.

Of course, Jesus may only be speaking figuratively here, but even if so, it reveals Satan's presumed connection with God, which is the same as in the Old Testament. On the other hand, Jesus is definitely portrayed here as having special knowledge of what will happen. After Peter indignantly denies that he will fail Jesus in any way, Jesus tells him that he will undergo and fail a threefold test that very night before cockcrow and deny any relationship with him.

Luke does not name Satan again in his Gospel, but we can doubtless infer his presence throughout the tribulation that Jesus soon undergoes. Unlike Mark and Matthew, Luke does not divide the agony in the garden into a three-part ordeal, but he does have Jesus comforted by an angel (Luke 22:43), just as he was ministered to by angels at the end of his trials in the desert in Mark and Matthew. Before and after his troubled prayer, he tells the disciples to pray "lest you enter into temptation" (Luke 22:40, 46), that is, so as not to succumb to testing.

Luke then shows that Jesus was subjected to three separate judicial trials: first, before the Sanhedrin, then before Herod, and finally before Pilate. No doubt we are meant to recall the prosecutorial role of Satan in Zechariah.

We can make a further inference: Satan's testing and judgmental functions can be seen in various of Jesus's encounters with opponents who question his actions. Why do you eat with sinners

(Luke 5:30)? Why do your disciples not fast (5:33)? Why do they acquire food on the Sabbath (6:2)?

Sometimes, however, Jesus forestalls objections from his enemies, who, we are told, are vigilant for accusations against him (which is also one of Satan's functions), as, for instance, when Jesus asks his critics whether it is lawful to do good on the Sabbath (Luke 6:6–11). We can see something of the sort even in the civil discussion that Jesus has with Simon the Pharisee, when he responds to Simon's implicit objection to the woman who had entered and ministered to his feet with her tears and ointment (Luke 7:37–50).

One could even say that Jesus is testing his host here; since Simon addresses Jesus respectfully as Rabbi, he seems to have passed the test. In other conversations, there appears to be a mutual testing. For instance, when a lawyer tests Jesus with a question about how to gain eternal life, Jesus responds with a question of his own: "What does the law say?" Jesus then commends his answer: to love God and neighbor. But the lawyer, "wishing to justify himself"—that is, for asking the question in the first place (in a sense to apologize for testing Jesus)—asks precisely who his neighbor is, to which Jesus responds with the parable of the Good Samaritan (Luke 10:25–37). We conclude that both sides passed their tests and were satisfied with the exchange.

In other words, we must not think of testing/tempting as the sole prerogative of Satan. Rather, it is basically God's way of checking us out in order to prove our worthiness. As we have seen, it was prominent in Scripture not only that God tested Job at Satan's urging, but also that He tested Abraham to the limit without any encouragement from Satan. In a way, any prayer of petition is essentially an earnest request to God to stop or refrain from testing us: not only "lead us not into temptation," but "give us our daily bread," and "send us rain," and "please stop the pain," and "make this angel of Satan remove his arrow," and "let this chalice pass from me."

* * *

To sum up what Luke has told us about Satan, we recall first of all, the original conversation presented to us after Jesus's fasting in the desert, where Satan affirms that he has been assigned to rule the kingdoms of the world. The nature of his rule can be partially surmised from the very challenges that he puts to Jesus. He suggests certain courses of action, in order to assess the subject's moral character. He is able to cite Scripture and offer interpretations for the meaning of what is found there (Luke 4).

When he speaks of Satan to his disciples, Jesus acknowledges his position of power, and also his hostile personality—he is the enemy. The disciples should resist him and do good, which will hasten his fall from power (Luke 10). Even so, because Satan's power remains strong (Luke 11), the apostles must do their best to rescue persons from him by way of faith (Acts 26) and by undoing the physical hardships, such as demonic parasites, he has imposed upon people (Luke 13, Acts 10).

One must guard against Satan's direct urgings to sin, as when he is said to actually enter a person, for instance, as with Judas (Luke 22) and Ananias (Acts 5), apparently hopeless cases, for they are given no chance to repent, unlike Peter and the other apostles (Luke 22) as well as Paul (Acts 26), who are rescued through the active intervention of Jesus himself.

Chapter 19

John's Devil: behind Cain and all sinners

It is striking that the last of the four evangelists, John, refers specifically to Satan/Devil only four times in his Gospel, three times in reference to Judas, and once in the discourse of Jesus, when Jesus addresses a hostile audience in Jerusalem. But John does refer to him in other terms elsewhere, as we shall see in the next chapter.

Let us begin with the Jerusalem episode. The persons with whom Jesus speaks are "Judeans," usually translated as "Jews." Construed as a geographical reference, the term is appropriate in John's eighth chapter, since Jesus is actually in Judea, but John uses it as well of Galileans who are in opposition to Jesus.

On this occasion, in the midst of Jesus's regular stints of preaching in the temple, there are many puzzling features, among which is his account of Devil. We are first told that Jesus is addressing those who had originally believed in him (John 8:31a), but it immediately becomes clear that they are now hostile to him and take offense at his words. When Jesus says, "If you continue in my word, you are truly my disciples and you will know the truth and the truth will make you free" (8:31b), they, offended at his implication that they are not free, cease continuing in his word, and, as the dispute escalates, Jesus tells them they are unfree because they are slaves to sin. Their main sin at present is that they are trying to kill Jesus. Furthermore, Jesus says, they are not children of Abraham, as they claim, nor children of God, because of their sins, but they have a different father. His explanation of who this father is, is

78

typically translated thus: "You are from your father the devil, and you choose to do your father's desires. He was a murderer from the beginning and does not stand in the truth, because there is no truth in him. When he lies, he speaks according to his own nature, for he is a liar and the father of lies" (John 8:44 NRSV).

The obsolete but still current interpretation of this account of Satan is that it refers to his identification with the serpent in the garden of Eden. As such, in a roundabout way, he is considered to be Adam's killer because he robbed him of his gift of immortality, even though Adam's actual death did not take place for another nine centuries. By extension, he is also thereby the killer of all of Adam's descendants. And, of course, his speech to Eve was a big lie.

Once we put this anachronistic explanation aside, we are faced with a difficult question: just what is Jesus referring to? What is the backstory that he takes for granted? Before attempting an answer, let us try for a more literal translation of the passage: "You are of the father of the devil, and you wish to do the desires of your father; he was a man-killer from the beginning, and did not stand in the truth, because truth is not in him. When he speaks the lie, he speaks out of whatever pertains to him, for he is a liar, and the father of it [i.e., lying]."

One way of elucidating this is to go back to the earliest appearance of Satan or Devil as an individual person, as we saw in the Septuagint version of the book of Job. Here Devil does not exactly lie to God but simply contests His favorable view of Job, and he predicts that under adverse circumstances Job will buckle and shout abuse at God. It is true that among the trials that Devil sends against Job are lots of killings of humans, since he arranges for human marauders to slaughter all of Job's servants and sends bad weather to wipe out his children. But this hardly justifies that accusation of "man-killer from the beginning"; rather, it would seem to be part of his ongoing testing of humankind.

An examination of the first recorded killing, and in fact, the first human death of any kind—Cain's murder of his brother Abel—offers a more promising avenue of inquiry. We will see below, when dealing with the so-called Epistles of John, that the idea of Devil as the father of sinners, with Cain as the prime example, was already in circulation. Later Jewish commentary that makes Satan rather than God the intermediary at Cain's birth—for "I brought forth a man with Yahweh," putting "I brought forth a man with Satan"—may also have had some currency in the first century AD.

The notion of Cain as the prototype of sinners may also help to explain the curious phrasing of our present passage, "you are of the father of the devil." We recall that the sobriquet "devil" (*diabolos*) was attached to Cain in the book of Wisdom (chapter 8 above). Perhaps Jesus is saying that Devil is the father of "the devil" Cain who committed the first murder and lied about it when he said, "I do not know where Abel is. Am I my brother's keeper?" In other words, those who succumb to the urgings of Devil become devils themselves.

In apparent confirmation of this notion is the treatment of Judas in John's Gospel. Just before the Jerusalem episode of chapter 8, in a somewhat similar exchange in Galilee, would-be believers in Jesus are first hopeful and then disillusioned. Their interactions with Jesus show a certain resemblance to Satan's testing of Jesus in the desert (in Matthew and Luke). But instead of being asked to turn rocks into bread, Jesus himself makes bread out of nothing in order to feed them, at which they pressure him to become their king (John 6:1–15), which recalls Satan's urging of Jesus to take over from Satan the kingdoms of the world. However, Jesus is indeed urged to make more bread the following day, and his response—"Labor not for the food that perishes, but for the food that endures into the life to come" (John 6:26–27)—recalls his earlier answer to Satan, "Man shall not live on bread alone, but on every word that comes out of the mouth of God."

A third episode occurs in the next chapter: the brothers of Jesus want him to go to Jerusalem, where his wonder-working powers will be better publicized (John 7:3–4). This corresponds to Satan's invitation to Jesus to make a similar display of himself by safely leaping off the temple.

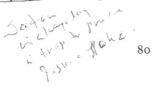

It is noteworthy that when Jesus calls Peter Satan (or perhaps, "a satan") in Mark and Matthew, it is because Peter begged him *not* to go to Jerusalem, where he would meet his death (therefore failing to fulfill the role that he was committed to). Here in John, on the contrary, Jesus refuses to be enticed to expose himself to danger and to the plots of death that are being hatched against him (John 7:6–8).

However, just before this, when the talk of material and spiritual food leads to Jesus's discourse upon himself as the bread of life, which alienates many of his disciples, he calls Judas a devil. Here is the situation: Peter, speaking for the twelve, has just reaffirmed his confidence in Jesus, who asks if they too will leave him. Peter replies, "Lord, to whom should we go? You have the words of eternal life, and we believe and know that you are the holy one of God." Jesus responds cryptically, "Have I not chosen the twelve of you? And yet one of you is a devil (*diabolos*)." John tells us he was here speaking of Judas, who would hand Jesus over to his enemies, even though he was one of the twelve (John 6:68–71).

We must ask ourselves how this betrayal of Jesus would merit Judas being called a devil. Clearly it is not because he is engaged in testing Jesus, trying to divert him away from his duty, as Satan tried to do in the desert and as Peter tried to do in deflecting him from Jerusalem. Rather it is because Judas is being enticed to sin, and he will give in to the temptation, just as Cain had given in to the urge to kill his brother.

John's further account of Judas bears this out. As Jesus and the twelve are gathered in Jerusalem to celebrate the Passover, John suddenly interrupts his account of Jesus's preparation to wash the others' feet, by saying, "Devil had by now put it into the heart of Judas Iscariot, son of Simon, to hand him over" (John 13:2). This sums up the temptation that Satan had been directing to Judas, to which Judas has already given in, and which he is about to put into operation, turning him into a satan or devil himself. As Jesus knew this would happen well before it did, so now he instigates the action himself: he professes to identify the betrayer among them by handing him a piece of bread (even though the others fail to catch on); and as soon as he gives Judas the bread, "Satan enters into him," and Jesus tells Judas to do the deed quickly (John 13:27).

Satan thereby becomes the father of Judas, and Judas becomes a satan himself, in the terms that Jesus had defined to his Jerusalem adversaries earlier, when he spoke of the first murderer, Cain.

Chapter 20

John's Devil as ruler of the world, already judged but still at work

John's Gospel shows affinities especially with Luke, but Luke puts the tradition of Satan entering into Judas earlier in the supper and introduces the idea of Satan's further testing of both Jesus and the remaining eleven apostles, after getting God's approval to do so; this testing plays out in the garden of Gethsemane and later. But in John, Jesus seems to take his testing by Satan as finished, and his success and glorification as inevitable.

For John introduces another function of Satan, that of ruler of the world. This was also an important element in Luke's presentation, as we remember, where Satan claims to have been given the rule of the kingdoms of the world (Luke 4:6), and Jesus has a vision of the sudden end of Satan's rule (Luke 10:18). John has Jesus bring up this role after Satan enters into Judas and Judas departs. The time is short, he says, for "now the ruler (*archon*) of the world (*kosmos*) is coming, and he has nothing on me"—because Jesus will do what the Father has commanded him (John 14:30–31).

Jesus had already prepared his apostles for this message, in Bethany, when he told them and the gathered crowd that even though his heart was troubled, he refused to ask his Father to save him from "this hour," for the purpose of the hour was to glorify the Father's name (John 12:27–28). He tells them, "Now is the judgment (verdict) on this world; now shall the ruler of the world be cast out. And I, if I be lifted up from the earth, will draw all to me"

(John 12:31–32). He is claiming that the result of his death will not only be the glorification of the Father but also a judgment against the world and its ruler.

It may well be that Satan's reputation had degenerated to such an extent by the time of John's Gospel that Satan himself, along with the sinners he instigates, is considered to be guilty of their sins, and will face a reckoning. This seems to be the purport of what Jesus says later to the apostles at the Last Supper. After I go away, he says, I will send the Helper (Advocate, Paraclete), who will accuse (*elenchein*) the world about what is wrong (sin), what is right (justice), and what the consequences are (judgment). The sin of the world is its failure to believe in me; I am in the right, which will be shown by my going to the Father. The judgment I speak of is manifest because "the ruler of this world has already been judged" (John 16:7–11).

This mysterious prediction is followed by a promise that the Helper, who is the Spirit of Truth, will lead them to the complete truth. But the truth of what Jesus says here will remain veiled through the rest of the Gospel, especially his assertion that the conviction of Satan has already taken place.

We recall that in the book of Zechariah, Satan was the judicial accuser, whereas here the Spirit of Truth seems to have succeeded to this position, since Satan has already been found guilty of malfeasance. But Satan can hardly be saddled with the guilt of sin in the same way as before, when Jesus spoke of him earlier, attributing to him both Cain's murder of Abel and the Judeans' murder plots against himself. Satan's guilt here must be something else: the guilt of blinding the world to the truth of who Jesus is.

However, even if Satan has been found guilty of various misdeeds, it does not mean that he has been removed from power. Remember, Jesus warned that "the ruler of this world is coming," even though he asserts later that he has already been convicted. Satan will continue in his role of opposition, as in Luke's portrayal. Nothwithstanding that he has received an unfavorable performance evaluation, his position as ruler of the world has not yet been eliminated.

This analysis is confirmed in the prayer to the Father that Jesus makes at the end of his discourse at the Last Supper: "I do not ask you to take them out of the world, but that you keep them from harm"—or "Harm," that is, Devil (John 17:15). This is the same prayer that he taught them in Matthew: "but deliver us from evil/harm"—or "the One Who Causes Evil/Harmful Things to Happen to Us." Devil and his temptations are still to be feared and guarded against.

Another aspect of John's Gospel that has frequently been aligned with his treatment of Satan is his dualistic imagery of light and dark. This theme emerges at the very beginning, in his account of how the Word became flesh: "In him was life, and the life was the light of men, and the light shines in the darkness, and the darkness did not take hold of it" (John 1:5). It would be natural to assume that John has Satan's opposition in mind when he speaks in these terms. If so, however, Jesus misses a good opportunity to make the correlation clear in chapter 8. Here, before connecting his opponents with Devil, Jesus says, "I am the light of the world. Whoever follows me will not walk in the dark but will have the light of life" (John 8:12); but he does not go on to connect the murdering and lying Devil, or devil (Cain), with the dark.

Similarly, after telling his listeners in chapter 12 that the ruler of the world will be driven out, he goes on to say, "The light is among you only a little while longer. Walk while you have the light, or the darkness will take hold of you" (John 12:35). This verb, "take hold of," is the same used in John's prologue, and once again, it seems like a lesson different from a discourse on Satan.

However this may be, Devil has received his due in John's account of Jesus and his mission.

PART 5

The rest of the New Testament

Chapter 21

Deutero-Paul of 2 Thessalonians: Satan and God working together

Apart from the Gospels and the Acts of the Apostles (a sequel to the Gospel of Luke), the New Testament consists of writings that are roughly characterized as letters, with an appendix, the book of Revelation, which is a collection of visionary descriptions.

We will begin with the ostensible letters that claim to have been written by Paul, which for centuries were accepted as authentically his; but in more recent times they have been judged to be "pseudepigraphs," writings that falsely claim authorship by famous persons. We could call each of these authors "Pseudo-Paul"; but instead I give their intentions the benefit of the doubt, and use the term "Deutero-Paul," or "DP" for short, that is, "Second Paul." There is a precedent for this when modern biblical scholars speak of "Deutero-Isaiah" to indicate a later writer who added material to Isaiah's original prophecies.

The first Deutero-Paul we will take up is the author who invented a second letter by Paul to the Thessalonians, probably at the end of the first century. This DP imitates the genuine letter by naming Silvanus and Timothy as coauthors. At the end, he speaks in the first person singular, as Paul does in 1 Thessalonians, but here in 2 Thessalonians he specifically identifies himself as Paul and calls attention to the supposed mark that he uses to authenticate his letters (2 Thess 3:17). This concern about authenticity is one of the chief reasons for *doubting* his authenticity.

89

We saw (chapter 10 above) that in Paul's actual letter, he closes with admonitions about the imminent return of the Lord, but gives contradictory accounts of his arrival. On the one hand, he will appear with great fanfare. On the other hand, he will come without warning, like a thief in the night. The effect of the latter style of coming would be sudden disaster for those who are in darkness. Paul's readers, however, are not in the dark but are children of light; nevertheless, they are not to be complacent but should arm themselves with faith and love and hope (1 Thess 5:4–8).

The new Paul, knowing that the day of expectation still has not arrived a half-century later, tells his pseudo-audience (Thessalonians in Paul's time) to expect a delay before the end and to expect a great struggle against opposing forces. They are to believe no letter from him that says that the day of the Lord is already here (2 Thess 2:2). A "Man of Lawlessness" must first appear, who, though destined to be destroyed, will cause great apostasy, and he will assume divine honors for himself. He will be "the adversary," *ho antikeimenos* (2 Thess 2:4). This is one of the ways of translating *satan* in the Septuagint; but whereas the satans of the Old Testament and Satan himself were adversaries against men, the Man of Lawlessness will oppose himself against the things of God and will assume divine authority for himself. The secret power of his lawlessness is already at work (*energeitai*, "is energized"), and will only cease when Jesus disposes of him at his coming (2 Thess 2:7–8).

What does the Man of Lawlessness have to do with Satan, we ask? We are told immediately: "His appearance is in accord with the working (*energeia*, "energy") of Satan, with all power, signs, and deceitful wonders and all kinds of false enticements to bring disaster on those who are ripe for it, those who are on the way to destruction, because they refuse to love the truth and be saved" (2 Thess 2:9–10).

But then, in a significant twist, the author tells us that God Himself is involved in what Satan and the Man of Lawlessness are doing: "And therefore God will send them an *energeia* of error, making them believe the lies. Hence all those who have not believed the truth but have delighted in wrong will be judged and condemned" (2 Thess 2:11–12).

Thus we see in this cooperation of "energy" the sort of activity found in the original and still principal paradigm of satanic activity, at the beginning of the book of Job, where God and Satan conspire to test Job by making use of human actors, namely, the brigands and marauders who deprive him of all of his worldly possessions.

The idea that God would wish to deliberately mislead people can be seen in the Hebrew book of Isaiah, where Yahweh orders Isaiah, "Make this people's heart sluggish, and dull their ears, and close their eyes, lest they see with their eyes and hear with their ears," and so on (Isa 6:10; the LXX version makes it entirely the fault of the people). We have seen Jesus and the authentic Paul speak similarly. Jesus talks in parables "so that they may look and not see, hear and not understand" (Mark 4:12). Paul says that the Gospel that he preaches "is veiled to those who are perishing," but puts blame on "the god of this age"—which may be a reference to Satan—who "has blinded unbelievers' minds, to keep them from seeing the light of the Gospel" (2 Cor 4:3–4).

The Man of Lawlessness is the only figure in the New Testament who corresponds to "the Antichrist" in later Christian tradition. The latter figure is an invention cobbled together from multiple "anti-Christs" in the Johannine Epistles, on the one hand, and, on the other, imagery and activity in the book of Revelation. But it can be argued that the Man of Lawlessness was the skeleton upon which this fantastic figure was built.

Perhaps a statement in 1 John was honestly misunderstood: "Who is the liar, except the one who denies that Jesus is the Christ—this is the anti-Christ, who denies Father and Son" (1 John 2:22). The real sense of the passage is that *anyone* who does this should be judged a liar and a counter-Christ, an anti-Christian. A similar sense is to be seen later, when the author says that "any spirit" (meaning opinion) "that does not confess Jesus is not from God, but rather is from the anti-Christ" (1 John 4:3).

To conclude, Deutero-Paul in his invented letter to the Thessalonians speaks of the coming time when God, Satan, and the Man of Lawlessness will cooperate in bringing unbelievers to their deserved bad end. But then he returns to the present and addresses his readers' present needs, praying for their hearts to be strengthened (2 Thess 2:13–16). Then, after asking for their prayers for him (3:1–2), he affirms the Lord's fidelity towards them, adding, "He will strengthen you and guard you from harm" (3:3). Or is it from "the Harmful One," that is, Satan?

Chapter 22

Deutero-Pauls of 1–2 Timothy: dealing pastorally with Satan

In the New Testament as it was finally decided upon, there are two bogus letters allegedly written by Paul to one of his coauthors, Timothy. They are now arranged and numbered as 1 Timothy and 2 Timothy, mainly because the DP of 2 Timothy claims to be Paul in prison in Rome and close to death, whereas the DP of 1 Timothy represents himself as Paul much earlier in his career, as having recently left Timothy in charge of the Christian community at Ephesus.

However, I agree with scholars who reverse the chronology and assume that the DP of 1 Timothy was drawing on 2 Timothy. One reason is that when he speaks of two troublemakers, Hymenaeus and Alexander, handed over to Satan for reformation (1 Tim 1:20), he does so in a way that assumes knowledge of their activities on the part of the intended readers.

So let us deal with 2 Timothy first. DP warns "Timothy" to avoid godless chatter, which leads people to impiety, like Hymenaeus and Philetus, who are upsetting the faith of others by claiming that the resurrection has already taken place (2 Tim 2:16–18). As for the coppersmith Alexander, DP claims to have been personally harmed by him (2 Tim 4:14). But DP says that he took no steps against him, merely relying on God to pay Alexander back for his actions; nevertheless, he now warns Timothy to be on the lookout for him, "for he strongly opposed our message" (2 Tim 4:14-15).

93

Earlier, after speaking of Hymenaeus and his fellow disturber of the faith, Philetus, DP goes on to warn Timothy to avoid "foolish and senseless speculations," which only cause rancorous disputes; rather, he should "correct those who oppose him with gentleness," in the hope that God will show them the truth, and that thereby "they may escape from the snare of Devil, who has held them captive to do his will" (2 Tim 2:23–26).

Significantly, it is Devil who is considered to be responsible for the upsetting activities of opponents; presumably Devil has tempted them to pose their skeptical questions, and in effect commissioned them to do the same thing to others, acting as his surrogates. The remedy is to engage these opponents in gentle reasoning in order to get them out of the net that Devil has trapped them in.

Now let us look at the DP of 1 Timothy. He takes a much different attitude to Devil. First, he stresses the importance of fostering a good conscience; failure to do so can cause spiritual shipwreck. As examples of such disasters, he singles out Hymenaeus and Alexander. But, rather than giving up on them, DP took corrective action: "I delivered them to Satan, so that they can be taught not to blaspheme" (1 Tim 1:20).

So, Satan now is not spoken of as ensnaring persons like Hymenaeus and Alexander in sins of slander and false doctrine. Instead, Satan is the cure, the one who will effect their reformation. This positive function resembles the one projected upon Satan by the authentic Paul in 1 Corinthians (5:5), where the incestuous offender was given over to Satan so that his spirit could eventually be saved.

In the Corinthian case there was an element of punishment as well as rehabilitation. DP in 1 Timothy may be taking this aspect of Satan's regimen for granted, as a necessary prologue to reform. Perhaps he intends his readers to think that he, "Paul," was somehow able to turn his opponents over to "the authorities" and have them convicted of some offense, like disturbing the peace, or involving them in some other procedure that would turn them around.

One indication that DP here is thinking in Pauline categories is that he refers to "Satan" rather than "Devil"—which was used in 2 Timothy. As we have seen, the genuine Paul uses only "Satan."

There is another reference to Satan in 1 Timothy, in chapter 5, which deals with domestic life. DP has been speaking against the idea of permitting younger widows to join the group of those who have sworn off further marriage, for fear that the strict requirements of this new life would be unsuitable for them and that they would become idlers and gossips. Rather, "they should marry, bear children, and rule their households, so as to give no occasion to Adversary (*ho antikeimenos*) for reproach." Indeed, he continues, "some have already turned back and followed Satan" (1 Tim 5:14–15).

If I am right in translating *ho antikeimenos* ("the adversary") as a proper name for Satan, it may mean that DP is referring to Satan's hallowed function of bringing accusations against offenders; then, in naming Satan by his usual name, DP alludes to his other traditional activity, testing and tempting persons to give in to his enticements, thus showing their true immoral colors. In this case, DP may be saying that such widows have not only failed to live up to the moral standards of the community, but they have given way to the temptation to abandon it altogether and remarry, after taking a vow not to become wives again.

Is it possible that in referring to both Satan and Devil, DP in 1 Timothy is referring to two separate angelic functionaries (and maybe a third, Adversary)? Possible, I would say, but not plausible. It is far more likely that he simply took these names as alternative and equivalent designations for the identical troublesome spirit somehow authorized to interfere in human affairs.

One of the references to Devil concerns the care needed in choosing a "bishop" or overseer, like Timothy, to preside over a Christian community. He must be highly thought of in the community at large, "so that he will not fall into reproach, and into Devil's snare" (1 Tim 3:7). We remember that the DP of 2 Timothy referred to Devil's snare, so perhaps his successor DP in composing 1 Timothy has simply repeated the metaphor, which most likely refers to a bird-catcher's net. Devil's victims are caught in it and held prisoner, being forced to follow the captor's wishes (2 Tim 2:26). This would represent the traditional diabolical ploy of entrapment through trickery.

But just before this, the DP of 1 Timothy brings up another traditional diabolical role, that of accuser. He says that a recent convert should not be appointed bishop, "for he might become puffed up and thereby fall into the judgment of Devil" (1 Tim 3:6).

Almost all translators have assumed that this means that such a neophyte bishop will likely commit a sin of pride and be judged, that is, condemned, in the same way as Devil was condemned. But when, we ask, was Devil ever condemned and convicted of pride? Answer: nowhere in the Bible! Maybe outside the Bible? If so, where is the evidence?

All such translators and exegetes have simply assumed that some sort of story of a proud angel, Satan, who rebelled against God, and was cast out of heaven, was already in circulation and well known to the writers of the Bible. We will see below that this explanation of Satan's origin would be formulated only in the third century AD, at the hands of Origen of Alexandria, with his interpretation of the morning star ("Lucifer") as Satan. It was only after this explanation was invented and read back into the Bible that "clues" to the story would be perceptible; and, unfortunately, they are still being perceived, even by sophisticated students of Scripture.

The closest that we have come in our review of the Scriptures to finding reference to a judgment against Satan is in the Gospel of John, in the passage where Jesus says that the Helper or Paraclete who is coming has convicted the ruler of the world (John 16:7–11). As we noted there, it is possible that this means that a judgment was entered against Satan. If so, however, the passage contains no suggestion that Satan was somehow condemned because of being "puffed up." (We should also keep in mind the likelihood that the Gospel of John and 1 Timothy were written around the same time, with little chance of mutual influence.)

It seems more likely that DP in 1 Timothy means that the puffed-up bishop will leave himself open to a judgment to be made *by Devil against the bishop*, in which Devil exercises his standard function of accuser, just as he does in the next verse (where one must guard against falling victim to Devil's reproach), and as the Satan of old accused Joshua the high priest in Zechariah.

After thus analyzing these two verses, let us read them to-gether: "[He must] not be a neophyte, lest, being puffed up, he fall into the judgment of Devil. And it is necessary to have good testi-mony from outsiders, lest he fall into reproach and Devil's snare" (1 Tim 3:6–7).

Finally, it should go without saying, but I will say it anyway (because it is never safe to underestimate the power of long-standing misinterpretations of the Bible): when DP speaks of the creation of Adam first and then Eve, and points out that it was Eve and not Adam who was deceived and who became a transgressor (1 Tim 2:11–15), there is no reason to see Satan lurking in the background (or Devil, on the off-chance that he is different from Satan), because Satan was not yet identified with the Eden serpent.

In reading the DP of 2 Thessalonians, we saw reason to think that Satan was acting in harmony with God's purposes, in mislead-ing persons who deserved to be misled. But in reviewing the DPs of 2 Timothy and 1 Timothy, we find little to suggest such coopera-tion; rather Satan/Devil seems to be acting on his own, under no visible direction or restraint from God.

Chapter 23

Another Deutero-Paul, to Ephesus:
Devil and the other super-powers

The epistle allegedly by Paul to the saints at Ephesus puts Devil into a new limelight, as a controlling force among the angelic powers of the heavens. Let us try to see how it happened.

There are many places in the Hebrew Scriptures where divine/angelic beings are shown to have responsibilities in the cosmos and over the earth. We have seen an example in the book of Job, where "sons of God" gather in the presence of Yahweh, the satan (or Satan) being one of them; and another example at the beginning of Zechariah, where patrolling angels ride celestial horses.

One very authoritative passage in Deuteronomy established that each country or people had its own angelic ruler: "When the Most High divided the nations, when He separated the sons of Adam, He set the boundaries of the nations according to the number of God's angels" (LXX Deut 32:8).

There are passages in the genuine epistles of Paul that may reflect this belief: for instance, when he refers to the rulers or *archontes* of this age who crucified Christ, and states that they would not have so acted if they had had proper understanding (1 Cor 2:6–8).

The DP who composed the Epistle to the Colossians elaborates on the notion of angelic rulers, calling them Thrones and Dominions and Principalities and Powers. Christ Jesus, the image of the invisible God, participated in their creation (Col 1:15–17).

Christ's death on the cross had the effect of neutralizing these spiritual governors as well as their human subjects (Col 1:15).

The DP who composed the Epistle to the Ephesians drew upon Colossians and modeled his own composition after it. Like the DP of 2 Timothy, he claims to be Paul writing from prison, but he does not say where he is imprisoned (Eph 3:1, 4:1, 6:20). At first, he talks separately about the supraterrestrial powers and Devil, with no obvious suggestion of a connection between them. But that changes.

In the first chapter, DP reflects the themes of Colossians by saying that when God raised Christ from the dead, He seated him at His side in the heavenly regions far above every Principality and Power and Force and Dominion, subordinating everything to Christ (Eph 1:19–21). It looks as if he may be distinguishing the heavenly realms from the atmosphere below, a distinction possibly verified in the next chapter, where he speaks of a single ruler (*archon*) of the power of the *air* (rather than the sky or heavens), who "energizes" or works in the sons of disobedience. The Ephesians were once among these offenders in the world, because of their sins (Eph 2:1–2). But God has now raised "us" up with Christ "and seated us in the heavenly regions with him" (Eph 2:6). Now, of course, DP is speaking figuratively, because, wherever Christ is, DP and we Ephesians are clearly not in the same post-mortem status, but are still here on earth, still struggling with the obstacles presented to us by the air-archon—whoever he is. Is he Devil? Maybe. Probably. Let's see.

In the third chapter, Deutero-Paul, calling himself a prisoner, addresses his audience as Gentiles, saying that he was commissioned to make known to them the mystery of Christ (Eph 3:14), and through the church (formed presumably by the Gentile converts) the word is to be promulgated further, "so that the manifold wisdom of God might now be made known to the Principalities and Powers in the heavenly regions by means of the church" (Eph 3:10).

So now it is clear that these spiritual authorities are in the heavenly sphere, like God and Christ and even "us," in our own way, but the Powers are clearly at a lower level. Just how the indoctrination of "the word" is to be made is not stated, but it is presumably through preaching; perhaps the writer means that the secular governments will be converted.

Our author returns to the contrast between the old ways of the Gentiles and the new ways of the Christians: there is to be no relapsing (Eph 4:17–18). He continues: "So, then, putting lies behind us, let us speak the truth to every man and his neighbor, because we all belong to each other. If you are angry, do not turn it into sin, let it not last until sunset, so that you will allow no room for Devil" (Eph 4:25–26). Here, then, is confirmation that the ruler of the power of the air is Satan, Devil. But Devil does not operate, at this point at least, by main force, but rather by sleight; he is ready to intrude himself back into our lives if we return to the old ways.

Eventually, however, Devil becomes a powerhouse, joined to the overtly hostile heavenly forces, as "Paul" produces lavish military metaphors of resistance:

> Finally, take on power in the Lord, rely on his might and strength, so that you can stand up against Devil's feints. For our conflict is not against flesh and blood, but against the Principalities and Powers, the authorities and rulers of the world, in the dark, against spiritual opposition and dangers even in the heavenly realms. Therefore, put on God's full armor and stand fast in the day of assault, with all precautions taken. Be steadfast, with the chainmail of truth covering your body and protected by a breastplate of uprightness, your boots ready to move with the gospel of peace, the shield of faith held before you to deflect and extinguish the burning arrows of the Harmful One (Devil), wearing the helmet of salvation and wielding the sword of the Spirit that is the word of God. (Eph 6:10–17)

The conflict seems at once daunting and reassuring, especially since God Himself is brought in at the end. The Christian fighter seems at first to be in single combat with Devil, and then greatly outnumbered by Devil's cohorts, but finally back fighting only against Devil himself, easily brushing aside his flaming arrows and confidently using the unconquerable divine sword.

We must not be misled by the author's imagery into thinking that the deck is stacked against us (to use a less physical metaphor). It is all up to us; we can defeat the adversary with the means that have been given to us. Remember that, earlier, we were able to avoid giving Devil a victory simply by curbing our anger.

As in dealing with the Gospels, I have been reluctant to refer to Devil here and elsewhere in the epistles as "the Evil One," so as not to pre-judge his character. He is clearly bad news, but can we conclude that DP assumes that, in some unexplained way, Devil, in mounting opposition to God's people, is acting in opposition to God's will? Perhaps, but there is no warrant to leap to this conclusion. We can just as easily assimilate Devil to the governing authorities, who need to be evangelized. We can also see him in the same position as the Satan of Job, conferring with God about how much testing the people need or can withstand. After all, we have been given much greater means to withstand attacks on our bodies than poor Job had, who had no breastplates or shields or swords to fend off Satan's reign, or rain, of terror.

Chapter 24

Hebrews: Devil as Angel of Death
(and ruler of the world)

The book called Hebrews was traditionally taken to be an epistle by Paul, but Hebrews itself makes no such claim; the writer does not announce his name and his intended recipients, as happens in all the Pauline epistles (whether genuine or not) that precede it in the New Testament. If the compilers of the New Testament had considered it to be a letter by Paul, they presumably would have placed it between 2 Corinthians and Ephesians, since the epistles ascribed to Paul are put in order of length, like the suras of the Qu'ran. Rather, it is placed as the first (therefore, longest) of the non-Pauline books. It is an anonymous exhortation to an unknown audience. But since it was obviously meant to be sent to the audience, it would certainly fulfill any commonplace definition of a letter, if not of a formal missive organized rhetorically in epistolary style, with only salutation and valediction lacking.

We have just seen that, according to the Deutero-Pauls of Colossians and Ephesians, Christ Jesus from the beginning was situated above all other spiritual beings in the universe, and when he had accomplished his time on earth, he was back in his original position, seated at God's right hand. Hebrews continues these themes, but adds much to explain the nature of Christ's mission on earth; he was for a time made to be a little lower than the angels, a human being, so that he might experience death like all humans, on our behalf (Heb 2:9). What would this accomplish? The answer

is straightforward: by sharing our flesh and blood and by undergoing death, he would be able to "destroy" the one who had the
power of death, namely, Devil (Heb 2:14).

"Destroy" is the way the Greek verb used here, *katargeō*, is
usually rendered, but it is a mistranslation, since there is obviously no question of Satan's somehow being annihilated. The basic
meaning of the word is "to leave unemployed or idle," and it is
used everywhere in this sense. Paul employs it to say how he "puts
aside" childish things when he becomes an adult (1 Cor 13:11).
The Jerusalem Bible comes close to the meaning of our passage:
God's Son "could take away all the power of the devil, who had
power over death"; the New Jerusalem Bible comes even closer:
"he could set aside him who held the power of death, namely the
devil." It is a question of *neutralizing* one of Devil's functions, not
of eliminating Devil altogether.

It is clear that Devil here has been assimilated to the Angel of
Death, a figure performing the role of a "psychopomp" or "taker-
away of souls" in Greek literature, which I will discuss below.
Meanwhile, however, we must ask what the author means by saying that Christ intended to deliver us from Devil's authority over
death, and succeeded in doing so. Obviously he did not mean that
we were rescued from dying; rather, he must mean that our spirits
were no longer at Devil's disposition when we died. As the author
tells us later, "There remains a sabbath-day of rest for the people of
God" (Heb 4:9).

Another function of Devil presumably left intact is that of
testing. The Hebrews author may be referring to it when he goes
on in chapter 2 to say that Christ was tested in what he experienced among humans so that he could help others when they are
being tested (Heb 2:16–18).

How are we helped by the experiences that Jesus had in resist-
ing temptation? One way is by realizing that "we do not have a
high priest who cannot sympathize with our weaknesses, for he has
been tested like us in every way, except that he did not sin" (Heb
4:15). In other words, he experienced everything except the suffering that comes from having failed the tests which he endured. That

is to say, he was able to overcome the assaults of Satan, and perhaps we are to see his success as having had and still having the effect of neutralizing Satan's power in this way as well as in countering his dominion over death.

Some of Christ's sufferings were connected with death, and he appealed to God as having even greater power over death than Devil: "In the days of his flesh he offered up prayers and supplications with loud cries and tears to the one who had the power to save him from death, and he was heard because of his humble devotion" (Heb 5:7).

We must conclude that Jesus was not saved from death in the sense that he did not die, but rather when he died, he was not subjected to the Angel of Death; the same will be true for those who follow his example.

The idea of Satan as ruler of the world may have been stimulated to some extent by his assumption of the role of Angel of Death, since death comes to all. In later Jewish tradition, in the *Great Midrash* (*Midrash Rabbah*) on Leviticus, when the Israelites promise to observe God's commands, He tells the Angel of Death that, even though He has made him ruler of the world (*kosmokrator*) over men, he must have nothing to do with the Israelites, for they are His children. This hardly means that they will not die, but that God has made other arrangements for their deaths, perhaps by tending to them personally.

There is more discussion on the Angel of Death in the *Great Midrash* on Deuteronomy in connection with the death of Moses. Rabbi Simeon reports an encounter that Simeon himself had with the Angel of Death, who identified himself simply as God's messenger. He tells the rabbi that he has no real power over death; it all rests in the decree of God. In a further pronouncement, Rabbi Simeon emphasizes that no man has the ability to tell the Angel of Death to postpone the fatal date set for him.

We will discuss this matter further in the next chapter.

Chapter 25

The Epistle of "Jude": Devil as Death-Angel, respected by Archangel Michael

The other New Testament writing that refers directly to Devil's role as Angel of Death is the Epistle of Jude, which also deals with the death of Moses. The author announces himself as a servant of Jesus Christ and a brother of James. He is not, therefore, pretending to be one of the apostles, "the other Judas" ("Judas, not the Iscariot"). But it is difficult to agree with scholars who say that he is referring to the Gospel account in which Jesus is said to have brothers named Jakobos (that is, James), Joses, Judas, and Simon (Mark 6:3), since he does not claim brotherhood with Jesus; but he clearly merits the name of Pseudo-Jude. He writes a "catholic" epistle, in that he addresses himself to all Christians.

His main concern at the beginning of his letter is to warn everyone against false teachers, particularly "blasphemers," that is, those who use abusive language, notably against angelic figures called Dominions and Glories, undoubtedly titles of heavenly powers. The author then cites an example of proper behavior: "When the archangel Michael disputed with Devil, contending over the body of Moses, he did not venture to assail him with injurious words, but only asked the Lord to reject his claim" (Jude 9). In contrast, he says, the human blasphemers slander what they do not understand, and go the way of Cain.

We can deduce from this episode that Devil was recognized as having a legitimate interest in the dead, and that it would have been wrong for Michael to insult him for putting forth his claim. Before we speculate further, let us look at some more midrashic traditions.

In one account in *Deuteronomy Rabbah*, when the Angel of Death approaches Moses, Moses seizes him and subdues him, and proceeds to bless his people, tribe by tribe (11:5). In the account attributed to Rabbi Meir, Moses disputes with the Angel of Death in a manner that resembles Jesus's encounter with Satan in the desert in Matthew and Luke. At the angel's first approach, Moses asserts that he has a prior obligation to praise God, citing Psalm 118:17: "I shall not die, but live, and declare the works of the Lord." The angel counters, "Moses, why do you give yourself airs? There are sufficient things in creation to praise Him; heaven and earth praise Him at all times, as it is said, 'The heavens declare the glory of God,'" quoting Psalm 19:2. Moses argues back, "But I shall silence them and praise Him," beginning his long hymn in Deuteronomy: "Give ear, O heavens, and I will speak; let the earth hear the words of my mouth" (Deut 32:1). The angel goes away, and when he comes a second time, Moses stymies him by pronouncing the supposedly unpronounceable name of God. This is in accord with another verse further on in Deuteronomy: "For I will proclaim the name of Yahweh" (Deut 32:3). On the angel's third try, Moses gives in, reciting the next verse (Deut 32:4): "The Rock, His work is perfect, and all His ways are just" (*Deut. Rab.* 11:5).

In the explanation ascribed to Rabbi Isaac, the soul of Moses struggles to go forth from his body, and Moses speaks to her, asking her if she fears domination by the Angel of Death; she replies that God will not permit it, citing Psalm 116:8: "Thou hast delivered my soul from death," and she says that she will go to the land of the living, as the same psalm says in the next verse. Whereupon Moses releases her, citing the previous verse: "Return, O my soul, unto thy rest" (loc. cit.).

The final account, attributed to Rabbi Johanan (*Deut. Rab.* 11:10), is the most suggestive. Here the role of Angel of Death is played by the angel Sammael (the name means "Poison of God"). He is identified as the chief of the accusing angels, and we are told that none of the accusing angels are as wicked as he, and he is invariably called "Sammael the wicked." However, he is clearly as much a member of the heavenly court as other angels, and takes orders from God. In other words, God seems to have no problem with him, and presumably his reputation for wickedness comes from his excessive zeal in bringing accusations against humans and enforcing death sentences.

It also becomes clear, however, that Sammael has a "bad attitude" among his peers. When it seems certain that God's decree of Moses's death will not be annulled, Sammael gloats about it to Michael, who is distressed at the prospect. Even though Michael responds by addressing him as "wicked one," he merely indicates that the tables will be turned: "Rejoice not against me, O mine enemy; though I am fallen, I shall arise" (quoting Micah 7:8).

But instead of commanding Sammael to fetch the soul of Moses, God orders Gabriel to do it. Gabriel, however, pleads that he cannot bear to witness the death of so great a man. Then God gives the order to Michael, who begs off in similar fashion. Finally, the command goes to Sammael. Moses demands to know who sent him, and Sammael replies that it was the Creator of all beings. When Moses refuses to comply, Sammael says, "The souls of all who come into the world are delivered into my hands." Moses replies by arguing that he is greater than other men. Sammael reports back to God, and God repeats His command. Sammael returns, sword in hand (think of the Angel of Yahweh, standing with sword as a satan before Balaam and his ass), but Moses attacks him with his staff and, pronouncing God's name, routs him.

Finally, God Himself speaks to Moses, telling him that his time has come. Moses responds, "I implore thee, do not hand me over into the hand of the Angel of Death." God agrees, and comes down Himself, along with Michael, Gabriel, and another angel, Zagzagel, and summons Moses's soul. The soul responds that she wishes to stay in his body, but God takes her away with a kiss. The heavens and earth weep, as does God Himself, and the soul goes to the life of the world to come.

Now, then, if it weren't for these accounts, we might be tempted to think that the tradition reflected in Jude postulated two angels of death, Michael and Satan, with Michael claiming the bodies of the just for honorable burial and Satan those of the unworthy. In light of what we have just seen, however, it seems more likely that Michael appears on the scene only because of Moses's exceptional character and that the dispute "about" (*peri*) the body of Moses is not "concerning" the body but "near" the body. It *concerns* rather the soul of Moses, namely, the question of who was to escort her to her final destination.

We can also conclude that, in the opinion of Pseudo-Jude, the character of Satan/Devil had not deteriorated to the extent that his bad intentions were taken for granted, because Michael is praised for not resorting to name-calling in the dispute.

We can confirm our reading of this passage in the Epistle of Jude by seeing what another pseudepigraphous book in the New Testament makes of it, namely, 2 Peter, which draws upon Jude. The author claims to be the Apostle Peter at the end of his life. He paraphrases Jude's admonishments against false teachers, and says: "They are presumptuous and willful, and are not afraid to speak evil of the Glories. But angels, though greater in strength and force, do not bring vicious denunciations before the Lord against them. These people, however, are like irrational animals . . . and revile what they do not understand (2 Pet 2:10–11).

By eliminating the example of Michael's restraint and his respectful treatment of Devil, Pseudo-Peter in effect treats Devil as one of the Glories that should not be treated with contempt or irreverence. Rather, the other angels should be imitated in treating them with the proper dignity.

Let me speak further about Sammael, who seems to have taken over the role of Satan in the *Great Midrash*. Among the midrashes on Genesis, there is one that shows Sammael in the position of encouraging the testing of Abraham and endeavoring to make him fail the test. As we saw in chapter 13 above, where the testing of Abraham was done by the angel Azazel, Sammael attempts to dissuade Abraham from sacrificing his son, but after failing in the effort, he succeeds in getting Isaac himself to plead for his life—but to no avail.

We note that in the *Deuteronomy Rabbah* account the by-name "wicked" is applied to Sammael, which is, of course, the same epithet applied to Satan in the New Testament. Let me recall my objection, explained in chapter 15 above, to translating it as "evil" and to speaking of Satan as "the Evil One": such a rendering suggests that he is the embodiment of radical Evil, as opposed to the infinite Good of God Himself. Calling Satan "the Wicked One" would be a far better alternative, if we can keep in mind that the "wickedness" involved is relative and situational: he is wicked because "he has it in for us," "he is out to get us." In some books of the New Testament, it can be argued that the author believes that God also thinks that Satan has transgressed the proper boundaries, and He will give him his comeuppance some day. But does any account suggest that Satan has somehow put himself permanently on the outs with God, and that God considers him to be Evil Personified? That would seem to be a conclusion of later readers of the New Testament, not of the authors of the books of the New Testament.

Chapter 26

Pseudo-Peter 1 and "James" on confronting Satan

The First Epistle of Peter purports to be by the Apostle Peter writing from Rome, which he calls "Babylon," to the leaders of churches in Asia Minor. He is confident that they are being protected by the power of God, through their faith in ultimate salvation, even though they must suffer through various trials in order to prove the genuineness of their faith, just as the purity of gold is tried by fire (1 Pet 1:5–7).

On the one hand, they are being tested internally, their carnal desires warring against the soul (1 Pet 2:11). On the other hand, they are undergoing a fiery test, being reviled for following Christ, but they should rejoice that they suffer like Christ (1 Pet 4:12–14).

We find at the end of his epistle that Devil is behind these trials and tribulations. After recommending humility, especially for the younger people, the author gives this admonition: "Be sober, keep a watchful eye. Devil, your adversary prowls around like a lion, letting out great roars, looking for victims to devour. Stand courageously against him, well defended in your faith, knowing that your brothers elsewhere in the world have overcome the same afflictions" (1 Pet 5:8–9).

This is not a question of "bearding the lion in his den," because the lion is on the loose, out in the open. Somehow, however, standing firm in faith will deflect his attacks. The nature of Devil's attacks can be surmised from the epithet "adversary," *antidikos*, an opponent-at-law, an accuser; that is, by keeping constant and sinless, no accusation will prove harmful against you.

So, what Devil does in a non-metaphorical way is to set tests, that is, temptations, for the faithful, attempting to make them falter and betray their faith. When this occurs, he can bring accusations of infidelity before the Court of Heaven and so "devour" them.

* * *

Another way of confronting Devil is advocated in the second-longest book after the Pauline (and Pseudo-Pauline) epistles, the Epistle of James, placed just after the longest, Hebrews. It is difficult to classify the author, who calls himself James, as Pseudo-James, since he does not claim to be any well-known person, whether one of the two apostles of that name, or James the brother of Jesus, or the James whose brother Pseudo-Jude claimed to be. Our James in this epistle addresses himself to all Christians, calling them "the twelve tribes dispersed abroad." Or perhaps he means Jewish-Christians, as opposed to Christians converted from paganism.

James's advice for dealing with Devil might seem to be the opposite to that of Pseudo-Peter I, who tells us to be on the lookout for a ravenous lion. Instead, James says, "Stand up against Devil, and he will flee from you!" (Jas 4:7). But in fact he uses the same verb of resistance, *antistēte*, "stand against." If we applied the same metaphor to Devil as Pseudo-Peter does, we would have to conclude that Devil turns out to be a cowardly lion, who has no power over us if we remain true to our principles.

James sandwiches his advice about Devil between two directives concerning our relationship with God: "*God opposes the proud, but gives grace to the humble.* Therefore submit yourselves to God, but stand up against Devil, and he will flee from you. *Draw near to God, and He will draw near to you*" (Jas 4:6–8).

Therefore, James indicates, it is our subjection to the will of God and our close relationship with Him that will prove most effective against Satan. The first statement, "God opposes the proud," etc., is an adage taken from the book of Proverbs (3:34), which the author of 1 Peter also cited before giving his directive about standing up to Devil.

A bit earlier, James made a similar point in terms not of Devil but of the World: "You adulterers, do you not know that friendship with the World means enmity towards God? Therefore, whoever decides to be a friend of the World is an enemy of God" (Jas 4:4).

It would not be beyond reason to suppose that James or other authors like him concluded that Satan was also God's enemy. But he does not say so, and, given the history of Satan as a servant of God who tests the faith of God's servants, it would be rash to assume any such conclusion.

James is preoccupied with trials, which is the first thing he speaks about: "My brothers, be joyful when you fall into various tests (*peirasmoi*), for the proving of your faith produces endurance and makes you perfect" (Jas 1:2–3). This is an attitude different from that recommended by Jesus when teaching the disciples to pray to the Father Himself not to lead them into any *peirasmos*, asking Him instead to deliver them from all danger—or from Satan's attempts to test them (Matt 6:13).

When he returns to the subject of testing a few verses later, James becomes very insistent that God Himself does not originate the testing—as if this would somehow be a slur on God's goodness. We might expect him to blame Devil for the testing, but he does not. Rather, he associates it with our own bad tendencies.

> Blessed is the man who undergoes a test (*peirasmos*) and proves himself up to it, for he will obtain the crown of life that the Lord promises to those who love him. But let no one who is being tested say that the test is from God. For just as bad persons (*kakoi*) cannot put God to the test, so too God tests no one. Tests are caused by a man's own desire, luring him out and seducing him; and when the desire has conceived, it gives birth to sin, and sin in turn, when it is fully grown, gives birth to death. (Jas 1:12–15)

In so saying, James is drawing on the biblical idea of "the evil inclination," spoken of in Genesis (Gen 6:5, 8:21) and later elaborated upon by the rabbis.

James returns to the idea of an internal struggle in chapter 4: "Where do the fights and disputes among you come from? Do they not come from the desires that are at war within you?" (Jas 4:1). This leads into the passage that we studied above, moving to the dangers of the World, and finally, the assault of Devil, which can be turned aside by a proper relationship with God.

Resistance to Devil will make him flee. Are we to think that he flees because he is fearful, or simply that he withdraws to return at an opportune time, as Luke tells us happened after Devil unsuccessfully tested Jesus (Luke 4:13)? We can only speculate.

James has stressed that successful weathering of tests produces endurance, and, after mentioning resistance to Devil, he goes on to point to the prophets as examples of endurance; but the only example he gives is that of Job: "Brothers, take the prophets, testifying in the name of the Lord, as examples of suffering evils and of patience. We call those blessed who endure. You have heard of the endurance of Job" (Jas 5:10–11). In looking to Job as a prime example, we can hardly avoid thinking about Satan, who started the whole tradition of providing tests for the faithful, to prove what they are made of.

Chapter 27

First Pseudo-John: Devil, Cain, and Devil's works

We come now to the three so-called Epistles of John. Since there is no interior acknowledgment of authorship, these Pseudo-Johns are pseudo-by-attribution-by-others rather than pseudo-by-author-claim. These epistles are letters without formal trappings. Only the first and most substantial mentions Devil. The writer starts out by speaking in the plural: "That which was from the beginning, which we have seen and beheld with our eyes and touched with our hands concerning the Word of life . . . we declare to you" (1 John 1:13); but he moves to the singular in chapter 2: "My little children, I am writing these things to you so that you do not sin" (1 John 2:1). It is estimated that he was writing around AD 100, but he speaks as if he was in on it all from the beginning (without giving specifics, however), so he is not completely innocent of pretense.

The next two very brief letters are by a writer who calls himself "the Elder" (*ho Presbuteros*). The author must know 1 John, because he picks up on the term "anti-Christ"; but since neither of his messages refers to Devil, we need not deal further with him here.

Here is what the author of 1 John says in chapter 2, when he varies his address among the youngest or newest members of the community (little children), the older or less recent members (young people), and the more seasoned faithful (parents): the children's sins have been forgiven in Jesus's name; the parents are knowledgeable about Jesus, who has existed from the beginning;

the young people have conquered the wicked (*ho ponēros*). Again, he writes to the children, because they know the Father; he writes to the parents for the same reason already mentioned, they know the one who exists from the beginning; and he writes to the young people for two new reasons—because they are strong and because the word of God remains in them—and also for the first-stated reason: they have conquered the wicked (*ho ponēros*) (1 John 2:12–14).

It is assumed by all translators that *ho ponēros* here refers to Devil (*ho diabolos*), for two obvious reasons: first, this was the usage of the Gospels; and second, because the author of 1 John will speak of Devil in chapter 3 (as we will see).

However, immediately after referring to *ho ponēros* here, he goes on to utter serious warnings against the world, *ho kosmos*:

> Love not *ho kosmos*, nor the things in *ho kosmos*. If anyone loves *ho kosmos*, the love of the Father is not in him. For all that is in *ho kosmos*, namely, the lust of the flesh and the lust of the eyes and the vanity of life, is not of the Father but of *ho kosmos*, and *ho kosmos* passes away and the lust thereof. (1 John 2:15–17)

Ho kosmos is masculine singular, like *ho ponēros*. Could not our author be speaking of "the wicked World" just before this? We English speakers, of course, are not used to gendered nouns and adjectives for non-living things. We cannot refer to "the World and *his* lust"; but we have to remember that this happens by rule in Greek and Latin and French and Italian and German and other similarly inflected languages; it used to happen even in English, back in *Beowulf*'s time.

But, of course, *ho ponēros* could refer to Devil here in 1 John, as the object of the victory (*nikē*) scored by the young faithful; and we will see it definitely applied to him below.

As noted earlier and just recently again, I have been reluctant to translate *ho ponēros* when referring to Satan in the Gospels as "the Evil One," for two reasons: first, "evil" has been exaggerated by philosophical and theological speculation to mean "radical malevolence"; and second, the designation makes an adverse *moral* judgment that may not be called for, if Satan is still thought of as performing court-ordered ordeals. But, as we will soon see, 1 John has such an obviously "bad" opinion of Devil that at least "wicked" (the term used in the King James Version) seems right.

If, then, *ho ponēros* does refer to Devil in chapter 2, conquering or overcoming Devil means that the young Christians have succeeded in not falling for the temptations to sin that he has presented to them.

But before 1 John gets round to speaking of Devil, just after denouncing the world, he talks at length of the danger posed by anti-Christs, persons who deny that Jesus is the Christ, that is, the anointed savior. Pseudo-John's readers know by the anointing (*chrisma*) that they have received what the truth is (1 John 2:18–27). He does not connect these anti-Christs with Devil (nor with the World, for that matter). It was only much later in the post-biblical world that a single malevolent anti-Christ with definite relationships to Satan was dreamed up.

In chapter 3, 1 John returns to the World: "See what manner of love the Father has given us, to be called and to be children of God. Therefore, the World does not know us, because it did not know Him" (1 John 3:1). But it soon appears that the alternative to being children of God is being children of Devil, drawing on the idea expressed in John's gospel of sinners becoming adopted offspring of Devil (John 8:44), with Cain as the most outstanding early example. Here is the story:

> Anyone who commits sin comes from Devil, for Devil has been sinning from the beginning. This is the reason the Son of God appeared, to take apart Devil's works. Everyone begotten by God who keeps His seed in him does not sin, because he was begotten by God. This is the difference between the children of God and the children of Devil. Whoever fails to do what is right and fails to love his brother is not of God. You heard this message from the beginning, that we should love each other—not like Cain, who was from the Wicked One (*ho ponēros*), and killed his brother. (1 John 3:8–12)

The usual translation of the mission of Jesus expressed here is to "destroy" Devil's works, but the Greek verb used is *luein*, meaning "loosen" or "untie," and the image that first comes to mind is the hunting metaphor of Satan as bird-catcher. Jesus's goal is to work against the temptations, the entrapments set up by Devil. The other use of the word *works* in the passage refers to the deeds of Cain and Abel, sinful and sinless, respectively.

It is perhaps possible that the author of 1 John is saying that Devil's works are sinful and "wicked." A bit earlier, he states the mission of Jesus as "bearing our sins" (1 John 3:5), usually interpreted to mean "bearing them away." If referring to past sins, it would mean taking away our guilt and punishment. But if it means future sins, then, of course, it would mean removing the enticements to sin set out by Devil. Are we to look upon Devil's deeds and activities as sinful? Perhaps. But that is hardly the main focus of our author.

There is one other reference to Devil in 1 John, at the very end, where it becomes apparent that the World is in his control: "We know that everyone begotten of God does not sin. If he stays God-begotten, the Wicked One cannot harm him. We know that we are from God, while the whole World lies in [the power of] the Wicked One" (1 John 5:18–19).

Our God-begottenness, of course, is not necessarily permanent; we can easily shift over to becoming "of Devil," by falling prey to "his works."

Chapter 28

John the Divine on Satan and the churches of Asia

A self-denominated John in the book of Revelation describes the visions he says he experienced on the island of Patmos. He does not claim to be the apostle John, and, even though he was very early on identified with the apostle John, the evangelist John, and the writer of 1–3 John, it would be misleading to call him Pseudo-John. Rather, he should be called John of Patmos, or, another good traditional name for him, John the Divine ("divine" in the sense of "theologian"). His book can be dated around AD 95.

The first section of the work consists of messages he says he received and now directs to seven Christian congregations in Asia Minor—or, more precisely, to the seven individual angels in charge of the congregations. The messages are from the resurrected Jesus in larger-than-life form, who is revealed now as the ruler of the kings of the earth (Rev 1:5). This is similar to the title held by Devil, which he offered to Jesus as a test, and which Jesus rejected as taking away from God's authority (Luke 4:6–8). It might seem ironic that Jesus in John the Divine's vision has assumed this position of power for himself. But obviously the author is working from different premises.

The first message of the Son of Man is to the angel of the church at Ephesus. We see that the angel has taken upon himself the satanic function of testing persons who claim to be apostles and has successfully exposed false claimants. That is, these persons have failed the tests/temptations set for them, and shown themselves to be wicked (*kakoi*). The angel is congratulated for his work (Rev 2:2).

It would be hard to imagine something similar happening to Satan—say if he had succeeded in proving Job to be merely a fair-weather saint, would God have been pleased with Satan? Or can we think that God commended Satan, after He gave Satan permission to test the apostles further (Luke 22:32), and he succeeded in making cowards of them all? We get the feeling that Satan enjoys his unsavory occupation (divinely sanctioned though it is) too much to be complimented for his accomplishments.

However, even in the case of the angel of Ephesus, that is only half of the story, because he turns out to have been delinquent on another score, namely, for having abandoned his first ardor and fallen away. He has become a fallen angel! He is told, "Remember where you fell from. Repent! Do the works that you did previously, or else I shall come and remove your lampstand from its place!" (Rev 2:5).

This is very significant: we see here an angel who has brought upon himself a fall from grace, but who is then given a chance to repent and make up for his delinquency. Would such a scenario be imaginable for Satan? Certainly not in the view of centuries of subsequent Christians whose minds have been closed to such a possibility, on the ground that once angels sin, they are beyond repentance and are stuck in their apostasy for all eternity. John the Divine's presentation here gives us reason to doubt such conclusions. On the other hand, we will see in the next message that his angelology is quite fluid, and he easily shifts between addressing the angel and speaking directly to the people the angel stands for. Perhaps we are to conclude that they are not real angels but simply personifications of the congregations, just as the lampstands are symbols of the congregations.

Satan/Devil himself makes an appearance in this message, which is to the church of Smyrna. Jesus tells the angel, "I know your troubles and how poor you are even in the midst of your riches. I know the railing abuse ("blasphemy") of those there who claim to be Judeans but are not, for they belong to the synagogue of Satan. But do not fear what you are about to suffer." (Rev 2:9–10a) But then the message shifts to plural, addressing the human members of the church: "Beware, Devil will throw some of you into prison as a test/temptation, and you will have tribulation for a period of ten days" (Rev 2:10b). Then the message reverts to the singular, that is, back to the angel: "Be faithful all the way to death, and I will give you the crown of life" (Rev 2:10c). (Obviously, he is not speaking of a real angel who is mortal in the same way that the humans are.)

Our author here uses both names, Satan and Devil, in quick succession, and we will see him doing so again later on. What is being said about Satan/Devil? First of all, it is asserted that he is behind the members of the church who falsely claim to be Judeans or Jews and who are slandering other church members. We can only speculate about what sorts of disputes are envisioned here, but the important point from our perspective is that Satan is assumed to be exercising his standard functions of accusing and trouble-making, the latter with a view to testing. The testing continues with the rough detention in prison. And perhaps this also is connected with Satan's role behind the secular authorities, as in 1 Corinthians and 1 Timothy (chapters 10 and 22 above), where delinquents are handed over to Satan for punishment and rehabilitation. In the latter case, the prosecuted miscreants at Ephesus (Hymenaeus and Alexander) were "blasphemers," whereas in Smyrna it may be that the pseudo-Jewish blasphemers were the ones causing other members of the church to be arrested and prosecuted.

The next message goes out to the angel of the church at Pergamum. Pergamum is said to be the actual place where the throne of Satan is to be found and where Satan lives!

Here is the text of the message:

> I know that you are living in the same place as the throne of Satan, but in spite of this you hold fast to my name, even as you did in the time of Antipas, my faithful martyr, when you did not deny your faith in me, when Antipas was killed among your people where Satan lives. (Rev 2:13)

Pergamum was the capital of the Roman Province of Asia, so
the suggestion is probably that Satan is seen to be exercising the
power of the Roman government.

Next, the Son of Man, now calling himself the Son of God,
addresses the angel of the church of Thyatira. This angel is doing
very well indeed, except for one point: some of his people are following after the false prophetess Jezebel, who encourages the com-
mission of sins. Her doctrine is defined as satanic, thus: "But the
rest of you in Thyatira who do not hold this teaching, who have not
learned what they call 'the deep things of Satan,'" are to hold fast
until Jesus comes (Rev 2:24–25).

What is the meaning of "the deep things of Satan"? It would
seem to be an ironic contrast with "the deep things of God" spoken
of by Paul (1 Cor 2:10), but it would hardly be used by those who
value Jezebel's teachings. It would seem instead to refer to the sort
of deceitful ploy used by Satan in his temptations, his testing of the
faith of the faithful.

Of the remaining churches, Sardis, Philadelphia, and La-
odicea, there is a satanic theme only in the message to the angel
of Philadelphia: he has done well, in spite of his lack of power.
However, his church is afflicted with the same kind of mendacious
pseudo-Jews that were causing trouble at Smyrna: they too belong
to the synagogue of Satan. But the Son of God will take measures
to make them submit to the angel, and he will shield the angel
from the hour of testing that will test all of the peoples on earth
(Rev 3:9–10).

The upshot of all this is that Satan/Devil is mainly visualized
as dedicated to his role as tester of the steadfastness of the followers of Jesus.

Chapter 29

Dragon-Devil's fight with Michael, symbolizing Satan's future dismissal as celestial accuser

The second and far larger part of John's "revelation" (*apocalupsis*) is a vast cosmic drama with a big cast of characters. Some of the preter-terrestrial characters who appear in these visions of the future are very sinister but have no overt satanic connection, though they may have been inspired by earlier manifestations of Satan. One example is "the Fourth Horseman of the Apocalypse," whose name is Death (Rev 6:8). We recall that Satan took on the role of the Angel of Death in Hebrews and Jude, but here Death seems to be a mere personification of a great plague, and so does his companion, Hades, the Greek god/personification of the underworld, who does service in the Greek Bible for the Hebrew feminine personification Sheol.

Another such figure is the fallen star Wormwood, who poisons the rivers of the earth (Rev 8:10–11), and yet another is the fallen star who takes the key to the abyss and lets out scorpion-locusts to devastate the earth; he is later identified as Abaddon ("Destruction" in Hebrew) and Apollyon ("Destroyer" in Greek) (Rev 9:1–11). In chapter 11, a beast from the abyss emerges to cause disturbances (Rev 11:7).

But it is only in chapter 12 that Satan returns, in the shape of a massively huge serpent, a *drakōn*. This word gave rise to our word "dragon," but it is misleading to use it without due warning, because our ideas of dragons have evolved beyond large snakes to dinosaur-like four-legged beasts often equipped with wings. The present *drakōn* is based on the great sea-serpent Leviathan that appears near the end of the book of Job (Job 41:1–34) and is famously described in Isaiah: "In that day God shall bring His holy and great and strong sword against *Drakōn*, the fleeing serpent, against *Drakōn*, the crooked serpent, He shall destroy *Drakōn*" (LXX Isa 27:1; the Hebrew text names Leviathan).

John's vision opens with a great sign or portent in the sky, a gigantic pregnant Woman clothed with the sun, having the moon under her feet, and crowned with twelve stars. Then another portent appears in the sky, an enormous red Dragon with seven crowned heads and ten horns distributed among the heads. His great tail sweeps a third of the stars of the sky to earth. Then he prepares to devour the Woman's offspring—who, however, is saved, snatched up to God's throne. Then a great battle breaks out in the sky, with Michael and his angels fighting Dragon, now accompanied by his own angels. They are defeated, there is no place left for them in the sky (or heaven), and they are cast down to the earth. It is only now that Dragon is identified as "the huge *drakōn*, the serpent, the ancient one, who is called Devil and Satan, deceiving the whole inhabited world" (Rev 12:9).

An announcement comes immediately from the heaven telling the meaning of this defeat; but, before studying it, we should note that the defeat is also a part of the conflict between Dragon and the Woman. When Dragon sees that he is on the earth, he pursues the Woman into the wilderness and tries to drown her with a great flood of water from his mouth; but the now personified Earth helps her by swallowing the water, and the enraged Dragon goes to war with the rest of her offspring, namely, those who keep the commandments and who are vouched for by Jesus (Rev 12:13–17).

The most common patristic and medieval interpretation of "the old serpent deceiving the whole world" was not as a reference to the great sea monster Leviathan, and to ongoing and future deception, but as an identification of Satan with the serpent in the garden of Eden who convinced Eve to eat the forbidden fruit. It also became common to identify the pregnant woman with the Virgin

Mary, as the descendant of Eve whose offspring was to encounter, not the offspring of the serpent, but the very Devil-Serpent himself who deceived Eve.

Although modern scholars have abandoned the identification of the portentous woman with Mary (without coming to any firm conclusion about what she is supposed to represent), they still cling to the idea that John the Divine meant to identify Satan with the Eden serpent, in spite of the obvious point that the latter was just the prototype of normal-sized serpents, and in spite of the inappropriateness of the description, "leading astray the whole inhabited world"—hardly the same thing as deceiving the first woman. True, it could be (and would be) taken to refer to Devil's ongoing activity, beginning with Eve and continuing thereafter, *attempting* to deceive all that he could. But its most obvious meaning is that it refers to what Devil will do more than a thousand years in the future, *actually* deceiving all of the nations in the four quarters of the earth (Rev 20:8), as we will see in the next chapter.

Now let us hear the announcement that interrupts this fantastic vision, with an explanation of the actual meaning of the battle between Michael and Satan:

> And I heard a great voice from heaven saying:
> "Now has come the salvation and the power and the kingdom of our God and the authority of His Christ. *For the accuser of our brothers, who has been accusing them day and night before our God, has been cast down!* They have overcome him by the blood of the Lamb and by their own testimony, not clinging to their life in the face of death. Rejoice, therefore, O heavens, and all you who dwell therein.
> "But woe to all of the inhabitants of the earth and sea, because Devil has come down among you in a great rage, for he knows that he has but a short time." (Rev 12:10–12)

The significance of this announcement cannot be stressed enough. The most important point to observe is that Devil is still in heaven accusing humans in the presence of God, and will only be ousted from his position in the divine court when the visionary encounter takes place in the future—after a sufficient number of martyrs have suffered for their faith. He has been in this position ever since he was first seen in the vision of Zechariah, where he was accusing Joshua the high priest and all the other priests.

It seems hardly likely that John wishes us to believe that Satan holds and has held this position in the divine court while in his monster serpentine form, seven heads and ten horns and all. There is a difference between reality and "things that must happen after this," things seen "in the spirit" (Rev 4:1–2).

Readers of John the Divine's visions over later centuries (but not at the beginning) have in general taken his future-telling very seriously, as authentic forecasts inspired by God of what God has predestined to happen, rather than as moral pronouncements on the present state of the world. They have done the same with the Old Testament prophets like Isaiah and Daniel, and changed the original meaning of prophecy, "speaking out," to "predicting." But in the case of the battle between Michael and Dragon, many interpreters will ignore the plain-spoken explanation in the text and take it to be an account of a rebellion of Satan and like-minded angels before the beginning of time (see chapter 33 below on the aftermath of Origen's invention of Lucifer). A similar interpretation would be given to Jesus's vision of Satan's fall "like lightning" (Luke 10:18), as noted in chapter 16 above.

Chapter 30

Dragon-Devil's still-more-future prospects:
1) dealings with other symbolic beasts
2) confinement in the abyss for a thousand years
3) success as deceiver of the whole world
4) final jettison, with Hades, Death, and sinners,
into the lake of fire

We saw that the first thing that Dragon-Devil will do after falling to earth is to pursue his mysterious female adversary. But the offspring that he was waiting to attack is gone, safely removed up into heaven and not to be heard of again. Now, however, it is revealed that the Woman has other children, whom Dragon will attack; they are identified as those having the *marturia*, "testimony," of Jesus Christ; they are ready to be witnesses, "martyrs," themselves.

The drama now shifts, as Dragon stations himself at the edge of the sea. John witnesses another monster still further in the future, a beast who emerges out of the sea, who, like Dragon, has seven heads and ten horns, but he does Dragon one better in having a crown for each of the horns. The heads themselves are covered with blasphemous names or slogans. Rather than being a Leviathan-like sea-serpent/dragon, as we might expect, coming as he does from the sea, this beast has distinctly mammalian characteristics, looking in general like a leopard, with the feet of a bear and the mouth of a lion (Rev 13:1–2).

Dragon bestows his power on this Beast from the Sea, and one of the latter's heads, previously wounded to the death (by a sword, we find out later) heals itself, and the whole world looks on in amazement. Everyone worships Dragon, and also Beast from the Sea, regarding him as invincible. Beast from the Sea is given (by Dragon?) a voice to blaspheme God and the saints for forty-two months and to overcome the saints, while being worshipped by all earth-dwellers whose names are not written in the Lamb's book of life (Rev 13:2–8, 14).

The next scene in this visionary drama is the emergence of another beast, this time from the earth, having only two horns, like the horns of a lamb, but with the voice of a dragon. This new monster, Beast from the Earth, exercises the authority of Beast from the Sea, and causes earth-dwellers to worship Beast from the Sea, deceiving them by the many miracles that he works. He orders the people to make an icon of Beast from the Sea, and he makes the icon speak and order death for those who refuse to worship the icon. The icon orders all to have a mark of the beast (which beast is not clear) on their right hand or forehead before being able to engage in buying and selling. The mark is the number of a human, and John first invites the wise among his readers to calculate it, but then reveals it as six hundred and sixty-six (Rev 13:11–18).

As John the Divine certainly intended, it is all very mysterious, but a majority view early on and to this day holds that he is speaking of the Roman Empire, saying bad things about it and its future, but calling it Babylon, as Pseudo-Peter did (1 Pet 5:13), and predicting a bad end for the worshippers of the beast (Rev 14:8–11). One high point in the colorful action that follows is that a demonian spirit looking like a frog comes out of the mouth of each of the three main antagonists, Dragon, Beast from the Sea, and Beast from the Earth, the last-named now called the False Prophet. The frog spirits perform miracles, and gather up battle forces at Armageddon (Rev 16:13–16).

Suddenly another beast takes center stage, leaving Dragon and his two beasts on the sidelines. This fresh beast, mounted by a woman, the whore of Babylon, has seven heads and ten horns, which are all explained; for example, the seven heads are seven hills (think of Rome) on which the woman sits, and they are also seven kings, and so on (Rev 17:1–10).

This Babylon-Beast is about to ascend from the bottomless abyss and go to destruction (Rev 17:8), but it is the woman who is destroyed (Rev 18:1–24). When the battle finally takes place at Armageddon, the Word of God on a white horse leads the good side, and the two original beasts are in charge of the other side. The beasts are captured and thrown into the lake of fire and brimstone (not mentioned before), and the human warriors are killed by the fierce horseman (Rev 19:11–21).

Dragon-Devil, who has played no role in all this, suddenly comes to the fore. John tells us:

> Then I saw an angel coming down out of heaven, with the key to the abyss in his hand and a great chain. He laid hold of Dragon, the ancient serpent, who is Devil and Satan, and bound him for a thousand years. He cast him into the abyss and shut it up and sealed it over, so that he could deceive the nations no more, until the thousand years were up. But after that he must be let loose for a brief time. (Rev 20:1–3)

What will happen during the millennium after Satan is out of the way? We are told immediately: the saints who were martyred will rise from the dead; this is the "first resurrection." They will be priests of God and Christ, and will reign with Christ for a thousand years, and the second death will have no power over them. Just before this, we are assured that others who have died will not live again until the thousand years are over (Rev 20:4–6).

Moving on, we hear that Satan will be released, but now there is no talk of resurrected sinners; rather we are in a fully populated world again, with people ripe to be led astray: "When the thousand years are over, Satan will be released from his prison, and he will go forth to deceive the nations that are in the four quarters of the world, all Gog and Magog, numbering more than the grains of sand by the sea, and assemble them to battle" (Rev 20:7–8).

Only now is fulfilled the description of Satan as "the old serpent who deceives the whole world"—a far cry from the idea of the first serpent deceiving the first woman in the garden of Eden!

The great horde of fighters will travel from all parts of the world and encircle the camp of the saints and their beloved city (Rev 20:9a). Perhaps these are the resurrected saints who have been reigning with Christ for a thousand years, whom the second death will not affect. Sure enough, no fighting or danger occurs; rather, fire comes down from God out of heaven and consumes everyone (Rev 20:9b). Everyone, that is, except Devil, who had deceived them; he is cast into the fiery lake where his two beastly colleagues have already spent a thousand years, and where they will all three remain to be tormented day and night forever and ever (Rev 20:10).

This is a sorry end to the history of Satan in the Bible, who started out as God's minister of justice. From what we can surmise, in the view of John the Divine, there was never any saving grace about Satan. There is no account of how he became so bad, or why he will be allowed to do the bad things he did, including getting out of his thousand-year prison to continue his bad deeds. That is, simply the way he has been in the past, and will be in the future.

But we must remember the fanciful genre in which John is writing, where monsters stand in for real persons. Apart from the hint of reality in the interpolated announcement that Satan functioned as a long-time accuser in the divine court, the imagery is decidedly unreal.

Satan's dispatch into the lake of fire is followed by more unreal events in the account of the Last Judgment. John sees a great throne with a figure sitting on it. Earth and Heaven flee before Him—that is, they become personifications. So does Sea, who delivers up her dead. Then other personifications we have met before, Death and Hades, also give up their dead. Finally, Death and Hades are thrown into the lake of fire, along with all people who have failed to be registered in the book of Life (Rev 20:11–14). As a result, in one punishing body of fire, which burns but does not consume, seemingly a surface lake rather than the sort of underground realm presided over by Hades, we see a variety of inmates: real people (sinners), personifications (Death and Hades), symbolic beasts (Beast from the Sea and Beast from the Earth), and a mixture of real angel and symbolic beast (Dragon-Devil), all punished together. It is not the sort of discourse from which solid theological propositions can safely be drawn.

* * *

We have come to the end of our analysis of accounts and mentions of Satan in Scripture. Although our last view of him, in the last book of the New Testament, is extremely dark, the view of John the Divine must be weighed with the opinions of the various Deuteros, Pseudos, and other authors writing around the same time, that is, at the close of the first century AD. We will attempt a summary of all the biblical data in concluding chapters, but first, in the next section, we will look at some radical departures from the biblical data.

An important thing to know and remember is that the book of Revelation of John the Divine, as predicting a great battle with Satan in the future, played a minor role in the thinking of the earliest Fathers of the Church, who usually read the fight between Dragon and Michael allegorically to mean humankind's constant struggle against Satan and other evil spirits.

The main early focus of attention in Revelation was the idea of the thousand-year reign of Christ and the saints. Some of the earliest Fathers, like Justin Martyr, took it literally, but it became common to read it allegorically: for instance, as referring to the church on earth; any part of the narrative that is inconsistent with this is explained away. For instance, St. Augustine says that the incarceration of Devil in the abyss refers to his presence deep in the hearts of the truly wicked people. Devil's binding only means that he does not have as full power to seduce men as he did before he was bound, and as he will in the brief time he is freed in the future (*City of God* 20:1–8).

PART 6

Post-biblical developments

Chapter 31

Satan identified as Eden serpent
(Justin Martyr)

The early Christian writers were faced with the task of absorbing and systematizing not only the various events and sayings of the Gospels and the Epistles of Paul but also the Pentateuch and the prophets and the other writings of the Old Testament, explaining just how the advent of Jesus the Christ, the Messiah, was to be seen as a fulfillment of everything. Luke reported that the risen Jesus laid it all out to the two disciples on the way to Emmaus (Luke 24:27), but they did not write down what he said. Thus, his followers had to work it out for themselves.

The earliest writers after Paul and the compilers of the Gospels did their best, and some of them produced treatises that they passed off as compositions by Paul or by those who had actually known and been instructed by Jesus. These writings were accepted at face value—or at least a face value was imposed on them—and they were eventually authorized as canonical and inspired Scriptures, which in turn had to be explained and harmonized with what went before.

It is not surprising that various solutions, sometimes conflicting, were formulated for the same problems. One of the problems, the problem we are dealing with here, was how to fit Satan into the mix.

My goal in these post-biblical chapters is to pick out the most popular, important, and, specifically, most enduring solutions. By far the most monumental and game-changing theory was to see Satan as a rebel against God from the very beginning. This was Origen's invention of Lucifer. Another highly significant development was the notion that Satan destroyed mankind's happy prospects by enticing Eve to disobey God's prohibition. I will start with the latter idea, Satan as Eden serpent, because it emerged earlier than Satan as Lucifer, but not as early as everyone says!

There is a persistent and almost universal belief that the identification of Satan with the Eden serpent was already in circulation by the time that Jesus was born—specifically, as reflected in the book of Wisdom—and that allusions to it can be seen in various books of the New Testament. I have tried to counteract these perceptions in the chapters above, and I have argued the case at length in my biography of Satan and, most recently, in my article, "Adam Citings Before the Intrusion of Satan," in the *Biblical Theology Bulletin* in 2014. Here I will simply explain where the notion actually appears first, in the work of the Samaritan philosopher Justin the Martyr.

Justin was born in the year 100 in Samaria, in the new city of Flavia Neapolis (now Nablus) to a pagan Greek family. He studied philosophy assiduously, going through the Stoic, Peripatetic, Pythagorean, and Platonic systems until he was attracted to Christianity in AD 130 or so. He defended his new faith for the rest of his life and founded a school in Rome, where he lived and taught until he was martyred around the year 165.

Only three of his writings survive, his two *Apologies Against the Gentiles* and his *Dialogue with the Jew Trypho*. It is the last-named that is of most interest for his original take on Satan. But I should first mention that Justin explained the other wicked angels (that is, apart from Satan) as first having sinned by taking human females as mates, as explained in the *Book of Enoch* (itself a midrash on Genesis 6:2: "When the sons of God saw that the daughters of men were fair, they chose to take wives for themselves from among them"). Rather than being imprisoned and put out of action, as is reported in the Epistle of Jude (v. 6) and 2 Peter (2:4), these angels remained at large in the world to cause trouble, and so did their offspring, the demons (2 Apol. 5). (Justin skipped the part about the angels first begetting mortal giants who killed each other off, with their souls surviving as demons.) In this way he provided an explanation for the parasitic unclean spirits of the Synoptic Gospels. Furthermore, instead of explaining away the pagan gods as nonexistent, he insisted that they did indeed exist, but they were none other than the above-described sinful angels and their demonic offspring.

Satan, however, anticipated the other sinful angels in offending against God. For it was Satan that Moses referred to as the serpent in the book of Genesis, even though he identified him as the cleverest beast of the field that the Lord God had made.

How did Justin know this? Because Jesus said so! Let's listen.

During the course of explaining Psalm 22 (LXX 21), which Jesus prayed while on the cross ("O God, my God, why have your forsaken me?"), when Justin comes to the lion in verse 13 ("they have opened their mouths against me, like a ravening and roaring lion"), he first says that the lion designates Herod, who sought to kill the infant Jesus by slaughtering all the infants in the area. But then he notes that the lion has another signification:

> By the "lion roaring at him" he also meant Devil. Moses called him "the Serpent," but in Job and Zechariah he is called Devil, and Jesus addressed him as "Satanas," imposing a compound name on him because of the deed that he had committed. For *sata* [Heb *satah*, "deviate"] in the language of the Jews and Syrians means "apostate," while *nas* [Heb *nahash*, "snake"] translates as "serpent," if you render the word from the Hebrew; joining them together produces "Sata-Nas." For it is written in the commentaries of the Apostles that when Jesus came up from the River Jordan, after a voice said, "You are my Son, today I have begotten you, and this Devil immediately came to him and tested him, even saying to him, "Bow down and worship me," Christ responded, "Get behind me, Satah-Nahash! You shall worship the Lord your God, and serve Him alone." For just as he deceived Adam, he was hoping to cause some damage to Christ as well. (*Dial.* 103)

So, beginning with this folk etymology, Justin finds verification elsewhere in the Bible. Since he is conversing with a Jew, most of the proof-texts that he uses are taken from the Old Testament in the Septuagint translation. In the above passage, he refers, in addition to the Genesis account of the sin of Adam, to the appearances of Devil in Job and Zechariah; he finds another reference to Devil in Psalm 82:

> I have said, "You are gods, and all of you are sons of the Most High. But you die, as humans do, and you fall, like one of the archons." (LXX Ps 81[=82]: 6–7)

Rather than taking the verses to be God's address to angels, Justin understands them to be spoken to men, in effect reading the second verse thus: "But now you humans die, and fall just as one of the archons fell." He concludes, "Thereby the disobedience of men, that is, Adam and Eve, is declared, and also declared is the fall of one of the archons, who is called 'the Serpent'; and this archon fell with a great fall, because he deceived Eve" (*Dial.* 124).

Therefore, "the human race from Adam onwards came under the power of death and the deception of the Serpent" (*Dial.* 88). One way in which "the deceiving Serpent" carried out his campaign of deceit was to invent stories about Bacchus, Hercules, Mithras, and Perseus to parallel the coming of Jesus (*Dial.* 69–70).

But the prophecy that Moses records shows that Devil was cursed from the beginning (the Serpent will await the heel of the woman's offspring); and Isaiah prophesied that he would be slaughtered by a great sword (meaning Christ)—referring to Isaiah 27:1, the verse about the sea-serpent Leviathan that Dragon-Devil of Revelation was based on (*Dial.* 91).

Justin cites the book of Revelation only once; he says it was by John, one of the apostles of Christ, who prophesied that the believers in Christ would dwell a thousand years in Jerusalem (*Dial.* 81). But Justin undoubtedly found in John's descriptions of the great red Dragon, "called Satan and Devil, the old Serpent, deceiver of the whole world," a confirmation of what he himself believed, for he had no hesitation about identifying Satan not only with the normal-sized ~~garden serpent in Eden but~~ also with the gigantic Leviathan.

Chapter 32

Satan's resentment of Adam
(*Life of Adam, Qu'ran*)

Before proceeding to the story of Lucifer, I wish to relate a different account of the fall of Satan in connection with Adam, which had limited lasting effect in the history of Christianity, but which survived as the reigning story of Satan in Islam.

In identifying the Eden serpent as Satan, Justin was simply following what he thought Scripture said, as he could piece it together. Scripture seems to have said nothing about *why* Satan acted as he did against the first man and woman. No doubt Justin believed that the reason was obvious: he was a born troublemaker, and did it out of sheer cussedness, just for the hell of it, since evil is as evil does, and perversity needs no excuse; and so on.

Justin's later contemporary, Irenaeus of Lyons (d. 202), does give a reason for Satan's ruin of mankind: he resented Adam. But he gives no reason for his resentment. Cyprian of Carthage (d. 258) comes up with a reason that was to prove very influential: Satan resented Adam because he was created in God's image.

A fanciful work known as the *Life of Adam and Eve*, which survives in fragmentary form in a number of ancient languages, brings this theme prominently to the fore. It used to be thought, and is still widely believed, that this work originated in the first century AD, therefore early enough to have influenced the book of Revelation or even the Epistles of Paul. But the best authorities nowadays date it far later, around the fourth century AD.

The *Life* starts out from the by-now well-accepted view that it was Devil who by his trickery caused Adam and Eve to sin and to be expelled from Eden. Adam and Eve do penance for their misdeed, but Satan appears to Eve as a bright angel and convinces her to interrupt her penitential regimen, saying that he and the other angels have interceded with God to accept their repentance. He invites her to join Adam, where they can partake in the sort of food they once had in Paradise. But when Adam sees him, he recognizes him. I summarize the ensuing dialogue:

ADAM: Oh, Eve, Eve, why are you not doing penance? You have been seduced again by our enemy, who deprived us of our dwelling in Paradise!

EVE (*falling to the ground and lamenting*): Woe to you, O Devil, why do you assault us for no reason? What have we done to you, that you keep deceiving us? Have we somehow deprived you of your glory and honor?

DEVIL (*sighing*): Adam, all my enmity and envy and sorrow are because of you! You are the reason I was expelled from heaven and robbed of the glory I had there amidst all the angels, and cast down onto earth!

ADAM (*astonished*): Why, what have I ever done to you? We have never harmed you in any way. Why do you persecute us?

DEVIL: No, Adam, it is your fault that I was thrown out of heaven. When God blew the breath of life into you and God's own image appeared in your countenance, you were presented to all of us angels and we were required to worship the image of the Lord God in you, as God Himself commanded. I refused. "I will not worship Adam," I said. "He is inferior to me, he came after me. He should worship me!"

Other angels who heard me agreed with me, and they too refused to worship Adam. Michael said, "If you do not worship as commanded, the Lord God will be angered against you!" I said, "Let Him be angered! I will set my throne above the stars of heaven and will be like the Most High!"

But as soon as I said this, God in His wrath forced me and my angels out of our glory. It was all because of you that we were thrown down into this world. Our sorrow was all the more grievous when we saw you enjoying such delights. So I deceived your wife and brought it about that you too should be expelled from your joys, in the same way that I was cast out of my glory.

We note that Devil is made to pronounce the boast made by the Morning Star (*Lucifer* in Latin) in Isaiah 14:12, which had already inspired Origen of Alexandria to produce a much different account of Satan's fall, as we will see in the next chapter.

One version of the *Life of Adam and Eve* comes to grips with facts of the Genesis story, which clearly says that it was one of the animals created by God after He created Adam, namely, the serpent, who deceived Eve. The explanation given is that it was Satan who enticed the serpent to act as he did. He approached the serpent and asked him why he demeaned himself as he did, for he was the wisest of all animals, and yet he did obeisance to Adam and was required to eat weeds rather than the fruit of the garden. He then proposed that they work together to expel Adam and Eve from the garden. He allayed the serpent's fears about the Lord's wrath by saying that he (the serpent) would only be the vessel for Satan's words speaking through him.

* * *

This account for Satan's fall because of Adam found a great deal of favor in many works, but in none so much as in the Qu'ran, where it is retold again and again, in ten different chapters (suras).

Just as in English the Greek *Diabolos* was transformed to "Devil," so in Arabic it became "Iblis." The scenario is much the same in all of the accounts: Adam is created in the image of Allah, and Allah orders the angels to bow down before this new creature. Iblis refuses, as in the *Life of Adam*, but whereas in the original account Devil based his superiority on having been created before Adam, Iblis also alleges that he was made out of a superior element, namely fire, whereas Adam was formed out of clay (sura 7:12). Although Iblis is usually called an angel, in one sura he himself states that he belongs to the lower rank of creatures called the Jinns (sura 18:50), in both cases, creatures made from fire.

Allah ordered Iblis to be cast out of heaven and sent to hell, but Iblis pleaded to have the second half of his punishment (going to hell) postponed until Judgment Day. Allah relented, and Iblis remained on earth, now called Satan (Shaitan), where he proceeded to destroy the prospects of Adam and his progeny (sura 7:27).

All told, Satan plays a rather minor role in the Qu'ran and later Islam, and the same is true of later Jewish tradition.

Among Christian writers, the idea of Satan's resentment against Adam survived, but in a different context: Satan did not fall because he objected to Adam, but rather, after falling for another reason (namely, pride), he came to resent the human couple that God created.

Chapter 33

Satan-as-Lucifer falls out of pride, not because of Adam (Origen)

After the identification of Satan with the serpent in the garden of Eden, the next great transformation of the biblical Devil was the idea that he rebelled against God out of pride and was accordingly cast out of heaven. I lay this transformation at the feet of the Egyptian Christian writer Origen of Alexandria, who died around the year 254.

Origen's early thinking about this matter can be seen in his treatise *First Principles*, on the fundamental nature of the cosmos, which he compiled in the 220s. Unfortunately, the work exists as a whole only in the Latin translation of Rufinus of Aquileia, who admitted to editing away various of Origen's positions which were felt to be less than orthodox. But there is no reason to think that the account of how angels arrived at their fallen state was altered from his original views.

In reading the Scriptures, Origen was always on the alert to find hidden meanings, which could be brought to light by perceiving certain clues. One passage that caught his attention was in the midst of a long tirade by the prophet Isaiah against the king of Babylon. In chapter 14, the prophet tells of the joy that will follow when the Israelites, who have been held captive for so long in Babylon, will be finally released, and their captor will be humiliated. The king's overthrow is presented thus:

4 Look how the slave-driver is finished! Look how the taskmaster is gone!

5 God has struck off the yoke imposed by sinners, the servitude imposed by the mighty.

6 His anger has struck down the nation with a deadly plague, a vile disease that has consumed all.

7 Only His silence remains, while all the earth rejoices.

8 The cedars of Lebanon cry out with delight against you: "Since you have been felled, no one has come to cut us down!"

9 Bitter taunts rush up from Hades to greet you, all the giants there who once ruled over the earth rise up to deride you, all the kings of nations, from their thrones.

10 They all shout in glee, "You too have been taken down, just as we were, you too are now numbered among us!"

11 Your glory has gone down to the realm of Hades, and all your great joy!

Rottenness will be your bed, and worms your cover!

12 *Look how the Dawn-bringer* (Gk *Heōsphoros*, Lat. *Lucifer) has fallen from heaven, after rising up in the morning!*

He has been crushed to the earth, he who once dispatched great armies to all the nations!

13 *Once you boasted to yourself, "I will go to the higher heavens, I will establish my throne above the stars of heaven,*

I will be seated on a great mountain, on the great mountain range of the north!

14 *I will ascend far above the clouds. I will be like the Most High!"*

15 But now you will fall down to the realm of Hades, down to the fundament of the earth.

16 Those who see you will marvel at you and exclaim, "Is this the man who shook up the earth, who made kings tremble,

17 who made the whole world desolate, who destroyed its cities, who kept all his captives in misery!" (LXX Isa 14:4–17)

Now, then, when Origen read these lines carefully, he agreed that most of them were indeed directed against the king of Babylon, who he said was none other than Nebuchadnezzar himself. But some of what appears here makes no sense when applied to a mortal human being. They are the verses that I have emphasized above in italics. Origen singled out particularly the line translated in Rufinus's text thus, "Behold how Lucifer, who used to rise in the morning, has fallen from Heaven!"

In *First Principles*, Origen does not apply these lines to Satan, but rather to a similar angel or "being of light," who, like Satan, fell from heaven. We know about Satan's fall because of Jesus's testimony in the Gospel of Luke: he watched as Satan fell from heaven "like lightning" (Luke 10:18). Origen notes that Jesus used the same expression, "like lightning," to describe his own future return to earth: "The coming of the Son of Man will be like lightning from the height of heaven and back" (Matt 24:27). Therefore, he concludes, this "Lucifer," like Satan, "once existed as light before he turned away and fell to this place, and all his glory came to dust" (*FP* 1.5.5).

A bit earlier, Origen said something similar about the passage in Ezekiel that denounced the prince of Tyre (28:1–19). Part of it, he explains, must refer to an angel whose duty it was to govern the Tyrians, but when wickedness was found in him, namely, an excess of self-esteem, he was hurled to the earth (*FP* 1.5.4).

There were other fallen angels too. At the very beginning of *First Principles*, Origen says, in Rufinus's translation, that, although the church teaches nothing more definite about Devil and his angels than that they indeed exist, it is widely believed that they were all angels [in heaven], that Devil was the first to become an apostate, and that he convinced as many as possible of the other angels to join him (*FP* pref.). This picture, however, seems to be at variance with what Origen says about the fallen Morning Star angel and fallen angel of Tyre, so it may reflect instead the consensus at Rufinus's time of writing (ca. AD 400).

Twenty years or so after *First Principles*, when Origen wrote his polemic *Against Celsus*, he concluded that both the Isaiah and

144

Ezekiel passages refer to Satan himself (AC 6.44). He says here and elsewhere that Satan's sin was that he was proud and puffed up, and as a result he was ejected from heaven. It was only later that, as the serpent in the garden of Eden, he deceived Eve with his promises, and, after Adam went along with her in her disobedience, they were expelled from Paradise (AC 6.43).

Origen was not the first to link the Lucifer passage in Isaiah to Satan. Justin himself seems to have done so in a treatise that is cited by a later writer, John, Patriarch of Antioch, but Justin applied it to Satan's *future* fall at the end of time. The same is true of Tertullian of Carthage (d. ca. 240), who, like Justin, believed that Satan's first fall was the result of his assault on Adam and Eve. However, Cyprian, Tertullian's slightly younger Carthaginian contemporary, related the same lines to an ominous new figure, the Antichrist, whom Cyprian helped to dream up.

Origen remains the first to speak of Satan's sin and fall before humankind came on the scene, and that is the view that survived through the rest of antiquity and into the Middle Ages and beyond. It had the effect of making Satan much, much worse than he originally was seen to be, and it turned Christianity into a highly dualistic religion, with the Principle of Good on one side and a powerful Principle of Evil on the other side.

Chapter 34

Satan gains control of humanity
(Augustine, Anselm, Aquinas)

One of the strangest developments to come out of the idea that Satan was responsible for the sin of Adam and Eve was that he thereby acquired rights over them—and not only over them, but also over all of their descendants, the whole human race. Part of the reasoning centered on the term "redemption" as used by Paul in Romans 3:24. The apostle says here that all humans have sinned and were out of God's favor, but He made them upright through the redemption that is in Jesus. Since the word means "buying back," and originally referred to re-acquiring a slave or captive by paying a ransom, what does Paul mean by it?

Paul knows nothing about any connection of Satan with the first parents, and speaks only in terms of abstractions or personifications. Because of Adam's sin, we were under the power of Sin (Rom 3:9). But Sin is not a real person. How can Sin be paid off? Later Paul will say that Sin came into the world because of Adam, and Death came through Sin (Rom 5:12). Death, however, is similarly unreal, all of which makes it likely that Paul's use of "redemption" is only figurative.

Once Satan was placed in the garden of Eden, it became apparent to everyone that Paul must be talking about Satan as the owner of the human race. But that raised a question: why would Satan want to sell back his possessions? One prominent answer was that he wouldn't, and therefore he would need to be tricked into forfeiting them.

St. Augustine of Hippo is the Church Father most often associated with the bad consequences of original sin, but on this point he seems to have been anticipated among the Greek Fathers. Specifically, Gregory of Nyssa (ca. 331–396) determined that the human race had freely sold itself to Satan, and, in order to get us back, the Son of God would have to become man, but keep His divinity secret from Satan. Satan was suspicious of Jesus, but after testing him in the desert, he concluded that he was a mere mortal who could safely be killed. This was a grave mistake on Satan's part, because he thereby imposed the penalty of death on someone who did not deserve to die. This unwarranted killing constituted an adequate ransom for the whole of humankind, and thus our "redemption" was effected (Gregory's *Great Catechism*, chapters 21–26).

The idea of tricking Satan would become popular in the West as well as the East, but it does not seem to have made its way to Augustine's attention. However, he did hold that Adam's failure caused all of his descendants to be in a state of slavery, all doomed to death and hellfire. He also agreed that Satan's hold over humanity was broken when he put an innocent man, Jesus, to death. This death constituted a redemption: Christ's blood was the price paid for us. Augustine speaks of Satan "accepting" this price, but it hardly seems the right word, since, as Augustine admits, it did not have the effect of enriching Satan but rather of binding him, that is, enslaving him, while releasing humanity from its bonds. He explains it in another way: Satan killed Jesus, who was not indebted to him in any way; therefore, it was only right that *all* of Satan's imprisoned debtors should be let free—as long as they believed in Christ (*On the Trinity*, book 13, chap. 15). All this is a twisted way of explaining the "buy-back" of Paul's term "redemption." The idea that one man who is wrongly treated can deliver all of the captives is explained by Paul's notion that just as sin came to all men through one man, so deliverance of all men came from another man (Rom 5:18).

* * *

Augustine's basic meaning is that Satan overstepped his rights and was punished for it, by being deprived of his possessions. Neither Augustine nor anyone else for centuries questioned the truly bizarre idea that Satan had these rights in the first place, until the turn of the twelfth century, when St. Anselm, Archbishop of Canterbury (d. 1109), insisted that Satan had no "rights" to humans. Instead, he seized control of them unjustly. Therefore, there was no need to pay a ransom to him, and none was paid. Rather, our redemption was effected by Christ, as representative of humankind, who alone could make up for the injury to God's dignity, being also divine himself (*Why God Became Man*, bk. 2 ch. 18a).

Unconvincing as it might seem to us today, Anselm's answer proved generally satisfactory, but in fact it left unanswered the questions brilliantly posed by his pupil, Boso, who acts as interlocutor in the dialogue (he later became abbot of the monastery of Bec in Normandy, a position formerly held by Anselm). Why did God have to "come down" from heaven to conquer Devil? Why could He not simply have commanded it? "Unbelievers could bring up objections like this against us," he says (*WGBM* 1.6). He goes on to insist that, since Devil had seized what he had no right to, God should have punished him for persuading his fellow-subordinate, man, to rebel, and taken away his unlawful possessions. And, though man deserved to be punished for his transgression, and while it might be appropriate for Devil to do it, Devil acted unjustly in doing it. God did not command him to do it, but only permitted him to do it. Boso says that God gave this permission "in His incomprehensible wisdom": in other words, he cannot imagine why He would do so. Nevertheless, he concludes, God should simply have used His power against Devil to free man from him (*WGBM* 1.7).

Anselm never responds to this objection; and the parallel question, of why God permitted Devil to provoke man's sin, is not even asked. Anselm merely remarks parenthetically at one point

that if God had not permitted it, Devil would not have been able to
tempt man (*WGBM* 1.19).

When the matter of Satan's power over humanity was taken
up two centuries later by St. Thomas Aquinas (d. 1274), he simply
said, "Man by his sin merited to be given over to the power of
Devil, by whose temptation he was overcome" (*Summa Theologiae*
3.49.2). That is, Adam and Eve deserved to be punished because
of their sin. But why was Satan given such power, or allowed to
exercise it? Boso's questions are not even asked. As he pointed out,
Satan was a participant in the crime and he too should have been
punished. It seems rather that he was rewarded for succeeding in
his nefarious enterprise.

Another unasked question: why should the guilt and punishment of Adam and Eve extend to the thousands and millions of
their descendants? Even in the old law, children were punished
for the sins of their parents only to the third and fourth genera-
tion (Deut 5:9); and Jesus corrected his disciples for thinking that
a man was born blind as a punishment for his parents' sins (John
9:2–3). Anselm simply states off-handedly that, since human nature was present as a whole in our first parents, it was conquered
as a whole when they sinned (*WGBM* 1.18).

It all seems so unfair to us nowadays. But such was the power
of Satan by that time—that is, the power of the mistaken idea that
it was by the will of God that a rebel angel would ruin God's plans
for humankind. That's the way it happened, and it was out of the
question to think or imply that God Himself was in any way being
unfair or unjust.

In the Bible, of course, Satan, as a divinely regulated investi-
gator, prosecutor, and punisher, is portrayed as having certain limited powers over humans. Testing Adam and Eve could easily have
fallen within his remit, but the Genesis account of the first parents
was slow to gain attention. It was only Paul and his follower who
wrote 1 Timothy who paid any attention to their disobedience—
but without connecting it to Satan in any way.

Chapter 35

Satan's future defeat by Michael shifted back to Lucifer's original fall

One idea about Satan that has been prominent in later centuries is that the great battle in heaven between Satan and Michael and their respective angels is not a future event, but rather took place at the beginning of time, when Satan was still Lucifer, and that his defeat constituted the fall of Lucifer and his transformation into Satan.

This idea, however, was a long time in coming. Let us look at how St. Jerome, the greatest biblical expert of his time, viewed both falls of Satan, at the beginning of time, and in the future.

When he comes to chapter 14 in his *Commentary on Isaiah*, Jerome accepts the entire passage on the literal level as dealing with the fall of the king of Babylon. But later, when approaching the same chapter from the anagogic or spiritual perspective, he explains how it applies to Satan. He first notes the difference between the Hebrew and the Greek texts. The Hebrew version has a direct taunt: "How have you fallen from Heaven, O Lucifer, who arose in the morning! You have plunged to the earth and been crushed, you who were wounding the nations!" (Isa 14:12). The Greek makes it indirect: "How has Lucifer fallen from heaven, who arose in the morning! He is crushed onto the earth, who before was sending to all the nations!" He was cast out of heaven because of his pride, and Jesus tells us that he witnessed it, when he said to his disciples, "I was watching Satan when he fell from heaven like lightning"

(Luke 10:18). Jesus goes on to tell the disciples, Jerome says, that, just as Satan fell out of heaven because of pride, the disciples can ascend to heaven by means of humility (PL 24:219–20).

Satan's future fall is predicted further on in Isaiah, in the first verse of chapter 27, which, as we have seen, deals with the Lord's slaying of the great sea serpent Leviathan with His mighty sword. This, says Jerome, is what John predicted in the Apocalypse when he wrote, "There was a battle in heaven: Michael and his angels warred against Dragon and his angels." An extreme sentence has been passed against Devil: he who in the beginning of Genesis was called the serpent, wisest of all the beasts, is depicted here at the end of the world as Leviathan, against whom the great sword will be drawn. Jerome's concluding remark is interesting: "Let those who say that Devil will do penance and gain pardon explain for us how they interpret the words given here: 'And he shall slay Dragon who is in the sea'" (PL 24:305–7).

Who were these persons in Jerome's time who took a softer line on Satan's fate? If they committed their ideas to writing, their works have not survived. But, earlier on, both Justin and Origen had moments when such an outcome seemed possible. Justin admits that sinful angels as well as sinful men could repent (*Dial.* 141), and Origen says that the goodness of God can reconcile all of His enemies (*FP* 1.6.1).

A common early interpretation of the Apocalypse's battle in heaven was to apply it to the time of Christ and later. One early commentary, associated with the circle of St. Ambrose of Milan, reads Michael's defeat of Satan as Christ's defeat of Satan by means of his Passion, and sees the angels of Michael as the apostles fighting against the other fallen angels (PL 17:877).

Another early commentary, this one from the sixth century, recently recognized as by Caesarius, bishop of Arles in southern France (d. 542), gives a similarly symbolic reading to the goings-on of Dragon and Michael. Dragon is Satan, and humans who follow his wishes are his angels, whereas Michael is Christ himself, and his angels are virtuous persons. The war in "heaven" is not literal; rather it refers to the constant struggle that takes place in the church. Satan and his angels would not have dared to actually fight in heaven, for we remember that Satan did not dare even to tempt one man, Job, without first getting permission from God (Homily 9; PL 35:2434).

The first writer I have found who placed the battle between Satan and Michael in the past, at the time of Satan's original fall, is the celebrated statesman Cassiodorus, who in the last half of his very long life (ca. 485–ca. 585) dedicated himself to compiling educational materials for monks, most of which showed no great originality. But in his notes on John's Apocalypse, he says that it is beyond doubt that the battle between the angel Michael and the Devil took place at the beginning of the world (PL 70:1411C).

However, Cassiodorus goes on to treat the conflict as if taking place much later. For one thing, he identifies the woman pursued by Dragon-Devil as the Mother of Christ, and he says that Devil's fall was met with great rejoicing on earth and sea, because his maliciousness had caused great suffering. Even now, Devil has great animus against those who persevere in their faith.

The first sustained treatment of the angelic battle as taking place in the distant past rather than in the recent past, or the present, or the future, occurs in the commentary written around the year 600 by Archbishop Andrew of Caesarea. He says that the description given by John in Revelation "can be accommodated" to both of Devil's historic falls: the one that took place at the beginning, when he was ejected from the angelic ranks because of his pride and envy, and the one that occurred when he suffered defeat through the Lord's cross and was "cast out": that is, when "the Prince of this World" was convicted of having exercised a tyrannical rule and was deprived of his power (PG 106:325).

Regarding the first fall, Andrew says, it is likely that God's angels under the leadership of Michael were exasperated at Devil's pride and arrogance, and immediately expelled him from their midst. That this is what happened is indicated by the words of Ezekiel in chapter 28: he was driven out from among the Cherubim and from "the fiery stones," referring to the other orders of angels.

Some of the early Fathers, Andrew continues, hold that Devil was cast out of heaven shortly after the creation of the world, but that he still retained some control of the air, which he had previously ruled, in conformity with what Paul says in Ephesians: our fight is with the "aerial powers." In contrast, Devil's second fall was not literal but metaphorical, meaning that his powers to afflict humankind were drastically reduced.

This vision of a great battle between Michael and Satan at or before the beginning of time, at Lucifer's rebellion, did not take hold immediately. For instance, the great English ecclesiastical writer, St. Bede the Venerable, who died in the year 735, interprets the battleground "heaven" of the vision as the church, and sees the encounter as Michael's constant fight on our behalf, which fighting will be intensified at the time of Antichrist (PL 93:167, 94:707).

Another Englishman, Alcuin of York (d. 804, and born in the year that Bede died) who became the leading intellectual figure in the court of Charlemagne, also believed that the battle is ongoing, referring to Satan's constant efforts to assail Christians. But the idea of the conflict at the beginning of time must have been making inroads, because Alcuin enters a strong protest against it: "Far be it from the hearts of Christians to believe that this battle took place when the Old Enemy and his allies fell from heaven through pride." Scripture proves that the war is here and now, he says, citing Ephesians on our battle against the heavenly powers, and 2 Peter on Devil as a roaring lion, and adding other arguments (PL 100:1154–55).

By the eleventh century, in Bishop Rufinus's treatise *On the Good of Peace* (PL 150:1602), the retro-shift appears as straightforward fact:

> The first and greatest discord among the angels occurred when "Lucifer, who used to rise in the morning," thinking to ascend to the height of divinity, said, "I will place my throne at the north and will be like the Most High." Then "there was a great battle in heaven, with Michael and his angels fighting against Dragon, and Dragon fought back, along with his angels, but they did not prevail." Cast out

was that great Dragon, who is called Devil and Satan, he
was cast out, I say, onto the earth, and his angels were
thrown down with him.

In the next century, Rupert of Deutz (ca. 1129), in his book
On the Victory of the Word of God, understood Michael to represent the Word of God Himself, who defeated Satan at that time in
heaven, and later, the Word-become-flesh "bound the strong one"
on earth (referring to the parables of the Beelzebub episode—see
chapter 13 above).

The most popular theological textbook of the Middle Ages,
the *Sentences* of Peter Lombard, finished around 1160, has a similar account: Lucifer's apostasy and fall from heaven is chronicled
in the book of Revelation (*Sent.* 2.6). The same is true of the most
popular of all medieval books, the *Golden Legend* of James of
Varazze (ca. 1260), in his history of the Archangel Michael. But
James also cites opinions that Revelation refers to the continuous
warfare between angels and demons, and/or to Michael's coming
battle with Antichrist.

The most sensational account of the great primordial war in
heaven, of course, is the one that appears in John Milton's *Paradise
Lost*.

Chapter 36

Lucifer fell not to earth, but straight to hell, creating logistical problems

There was still one more significant alteration of biblical data to be made before our standard modern idea of Satan was achieved. It was not enough for him to be blamed for an insane rebellion against God and also for causing Adam and Eve to sin and thereby to fall under his control. He had to be sent immediately to hell at his initial fall from heaven, and only then by some means appear back on earth, in the garden of Eden, to ruin Adam and Eve's life.

However, this idea of Satan being in hell from the beginning, along with the further idea of his being in charge of hell, was by no means an early distortion of Scripture. It took a long time to develop, and it is still not clear how it came about.

Let us recall what the Bible has to say on the subject: in Matthew 25, Jesus says that at the Last Judgment uncharitable people will go with the goats to the fire prepared for Devil and his angels. In Revelation 12, Dragon-Devil will be thrown down to earth to wreak havoc for a short period, which actually seems to last for a long time. In Revelation 20, we hear that he will be bound and confined in the abyss for a thousand years, and after his release he will succeed over a truly short time in deceiving the whole world, until at last he will be cast into a lake of fire to join Hades and Death, with human sinners to follow.

Isaiah's prophetic fantasy about the king of Babylon likened the king to an upstart Morning Star (Lucifer) who intended to place his throne above the stars of God, but instead fell all the way to Hades, already populated by the kings who had preceded him. Origen decided that the rising-up-and-falling-from-heaven section referred to an angel, eventually identifying him as Satan, because the passage did not describe a human being, whereas the going-to-Hades-with-other-mortals part did refer to the king of Babylon. It was the consensus of the subsequent Fathers that Satan fell "not quite to earth," stopping short at the smoggy air of the lower atmosphere, which corresponded to the dark skies spoken of in Ephesians, describing our fight against Devil and the Principalities and Powers.

We saw in the last chapter that some readers of Revelation interpreted Dragon-Devil's defeat by Michael to refer to Satan's loss of power at the crucifixion, and the thousand years of being bound to refer to his simply being somewhat constricted in his activities against the Christian faithful. Soon, however, in the sixth century, a very popular work called the *Gospel of Nicodemus* was given a supplementary chapter called the "Descent into Hell," in which Jesus puts Satan completely out of action. In an almost comic scene, Satan, after having arranged Christ's crucifixion, rushes down to hell to warn Hades and Death to be on guard against the soul of Jesus as potentially dangerous when he comes to hell. Hades berates Satan for making a colossal blunder, because not long ago this very man Jesus snatched away from hell a man named Lazarus, and now he is surely coming to take all of the dead away! Suddenly, the gates of hell are shattered, and Jesus arrives with his angels to rescue the souls of the upright and at the same time to restrain Satan. He orders the angels to tie Satan up, and he instructs Hades to keep him that way until his second coming.

This was not a scenario that was taken seriously, however, since all Christian writing, beginning with the epistles of Paul, was full of warnings of the continued presence of Satan in the midst of the world.

The notion that Satan as Lucifer was cast into hell immediately after his primordial defeat by Michael caused similar problems. Just when and where this concept of Satan's instant infernal punishment originated is difficult to say. Some of the earliest examples of it are to be seen in Anglo-Saxon biblical poems— which, however, are hard to date. Estimates range from the eighth through the tenth centuries. *Genesis B*, thought to be based on an Old Saxon poem, tells of the great angel who becomes proud and sets up a lofty throne, along with other like-minded angels. God casts them out, and they fall for three days down to hell. The leader, now named Satan, laments not only that they have been robbed of their places in heaven but also that they will be replaced by creatures made of earth, namely, Adam and those who will descend from him. Knowing that Satan would want to harm Adam, God has shackled him, neck and hand and foot, but Satan calls for a volunteer to fly up to Eden in his place. This happens, and the sad events of the fall of Adam and Eve's transgression and punishment follow. Thus, we see, the poet was forced to modify the inherited story by replacing Satan as Eve's seducer with another fallen angel.

There is a different solution in another poem, *Andreas*, where, even though Devil is bound in fetters of fire, he can still move about on his evil business, taking his fiery bonds with him. The same is true in *Christ and Satan*, where the other angels as well as Satan are chained. However, when Jesus comes down to "harrow" hell, that is, rescue the virtuous dead, he increases their restraints and thrusts them still deeper in hell.

In *Juliana*, one of the poems in which the author identifies himself as Cynewulf, the scenario seems close to that of *Genesis B*, with Satan staying in hell while the other evil angels accomplish his designs. St. Juliana is told this by a demon who has been pestering her. She captures him and forces a confession out of him; in complying, he takes credit for many of the obstacles that Christ met with during his life. He may also have deceived Adam and Eve, but a page of the poem is missing.

Cynewulf's poem, *Helen*, about the discovery of the true cross by Constantine's mother, changes the story: Devil himself shows up and explains that he can indeed do his dirty work in the world, except when Christ periodically locks him up in hell.

A still different scenario appears in a third Cynewulfian poem, *Christ II*, which resembles the account of the *Gospel of Nicodemus*: Satan and his angels did not fall to hell to begin with, but were only hurled there after Christ died on the cross and rescued the saints held captive there. Satan himself was then bound in chains of fire, and he remains there yet.

Peter Lombard in his *Sentences* is noncommittal on the subject. There are some, he says, who believe that Lucifer himself did not fall only to the earth's atmosphere but all the way to hell, where he was "buried," because of the gravity of his sin; yet others hold that he was bound in hell only after being defeated by Christ at his crucifixion; or, some assert—and this is a new idea—Satan's fall to hell happened when Jesus bested him in the temptation in the desert. Whatever the truth, Lombard clearly thinks, without explaining how, that Satan can still function in the world, for he goes on to say that he will doubtless have more power in the future, in the time of Antichrist, than he does now, for then whatever detention he has been constrained by will be relaxed (*Sent.* 2.6).

One of the best-known conceptions of the fallen Lucifer in hell is in Dante's *Inferno*, where Satan, left weeping and witless from the time of his fall, is so impaired that he could neither have seduced Eve himself nor commissioned another to do it, or to do any subsequent satanic activity, like tempting Jesus in the desert. Dante, of course, believed that such activity did occur and still occurs. We have glimpses of it in *Purgatorio*, when "our adversary" is pointed out, still in the serpentine form that he used in the garden of Eden (8:95–102), and when, in a paraphrase of the Lord's Prayer, God is beseeched not to let us be tested by "the old adversary" (11:19–21).

Unlike Dante, John Milton and other authors do have rationalizations about Lucifer's ability to act on earth while still undergoing infernal punishment. Milton explains that although Satan was chained at the beginning, God allowed him to operate on earth, so that he could spoil His plans for mankind and be punished all the more; but he gives no reason why God would stack the cards against Adam and Eve in such an egregious way. Here is what he says:

> So stretched out huge in length the Archfiend lay
> Chained on the burning lake, nor ever thence
> Had risen or heaved his head, but that the will
> And high permission of all-ruling Heaven
> Left him at large to his own dark designs,
> That with reiterated crimes he might
> Heap on himself damnation, while he sought
> Evil to others, and enraged might see
> Infinite goodness, grace, and mercy shown
> On Man, by him seduced, but on himself
> Treble confusion, wrath, and vengeance poured. (*PL* 1:210–20)

This is not a very convincing justification of the ways of God to men. But it was the best that Milton could do, given the impossible plot passed down from earlier biblical explainers.

PART 7

Conclusion

Chapter 37

Back to the Bible

Now that we have identified the elements of the post-biblical fantasies about Satan, it is time to sum up the authentic treatment presented in the Bible. (I refer to the above chapters in parentheses.)

The basic paradigm of the biblical Satan is that which is presented in the book of Job (3), in which God and Satan confer about whether and how much Job should be tested in order to ascertain his moral character. God comes across as easily satisfied, with no need for action, while Satan is skeptical and insistent that further evidence is required.

A New Testament example of a similar situation appears in Luke (18), when Jesus at the Last Supper congratulates his apostles for persevering with him through various trials. However, he says that Satan requested that they be subjected to more trials and tests so that they could be "sifted like wheat," that is, their impurities made manifest. Satan's request was granted, Jesus indicates, and it is a foregone conclusion that all of them will fail the tests. But Jesus says that he intervened with a plea, that at least Peter's testing would not be so severe that he could not recover and help bring back his brethren. This petition too was granted.

In the prayer that Jesus gave to his disciples (15), the final pair of petitions asks Our Father not to lead us into testing, but to free us from harm, or the Harmful One. If the latter interpretation is accepted, that is, as referring to Satan, it looks like another instance of the interplay between God and Satan on the need for putting us through our paces. Like Jesus in the case of the apostles, we should all implore God to moderate the pressure put on us so that we can more readily remain faithful. We have already assured Our Father of our good will, in promising to forgive those who are indebted to us, or who have trespassed against us. We also anticipated the final request about "harm," asking God not to test our virtue by depriving us of sufficient physical nourishment, but rather to make sure that we acquire our daily quota of bread.

In 2 Corinthians Paul presents still another case of temptation as a negotiation involving God, Satan, and the human subject (11). Paul says that he prayed time after time for God to remove the thorn in his flesh that was causing him so much torment. He identifies this thorn as "an envoy from Satan." Each time he prayed, God reassured him that the trial would not be too much for him to bear and that his strength of character would be sufficient for him not to succumb to despair or anger, or any other immoderate reaction. There was a good purpose for the ordeal: it was meant to keep him from being puffed up, from taking excessive pride in the privileged place he had in spreading the good news of Christ.

One of Paul's impersonators, the author of 2 Thessalonians, predicts that God will cooperate with Satan in bringing about the hardships that will come with the Man of Lawlessness (21).

The other chief paradigm of Satan from the Old Testament appears in the book of Zechariah, in which Satan plays the role of accuser against humans in the heavenly court (4). In accusing the high priest Joshua, Satan obviously has the evidence on his side, symbolized by the filthy clothes that Joshua wears, yet God intervenes and lets him off, dismissing as well the charges against the other priests who are waiting in the dock.

The clearest example of Satan as heavenly prosecutor in the New Testament comes in the book of Revelation (29), where Michael's coming defeat of Satan is explained as Satan's dismissal from his role of accuser of humans in God's presence.

In the case of Job, Satan was not able to make any accusation against him because Job had done no wrong, so instead he got permission to provoke him into committing sin. If Job had bent under the pressure and lashed out against the injuries inflicted upon him, then Satan would have moved on to his accusatorial function, named Job's sins, and demanded appropriate punishment.

Many of the references to Satan in the Gospels and Epistles detail the sort of tests and trials he brings to bear on the subjects of his attention, with the primary case being his personal appearance in testing Jesus in the desert (13, 14, 16). One of his methods is to put obstacles in the way, as Paul complains to the Thessalonians (10). He prays that his disciples in Rome will be able to trample over such obstacles of Satan (12). Jesus rebukes Peter as a satanic roadblock, a "scandal" (14), a description that harks back to the episode in Numbers when the Angel of Yahweh appeared as a satan in the road to prevent Balaam from proceeding (2).

Satan's appearance in Job indicates that he had legitimate jurisdiction over humankind: his function involved patrolling the earth (3). Satan claims to Jesus in the desert that the rule of the kingdoms of the world had been granted to him, and Jesus later says that his rule will come to an end—he will fall like lightning (16). In John's Gospel, Jesus says the same thing: the ruler of the world will be cast out (20). In Hebrews and in Jude we hear that Satan's jurisdiction extends over the power of death (24, 25), sometimes assigned to a specific "angel of death."

In Paul's view, Satan also controls the secular government's functions, not just the negative procedures of conviction and punishment but also rehabilitation (10); one of Paul's imitators, the author of the First Epistle to Timothy, has a similar conception (22). This fits with the positive purpose of Satan's affliction of Paul with the thorn in his flesh, to prevent his becoming too full of himself (11).

In the stylized debate that Jesus has with Satan in Matthew and Luke (14, 16), Jesus treats Satan with seeming courtesy. He accepts his claim to have the rule over the kingdoms of the world, and he readily accedes to be taken up on high and shown these kingdoms in all their glory; he also permits Satan to take him to the top of the temple, and, presumably, back to the desert. True, he dismisses Satan brusquely at the end, but this dismissal does not entirely negate the respectful impression given in the previous episodes.

Another New Testament author, the writer of the Epistle of Jude, makes a specific point of calling for respectful treatment of Satan (25). The same cannot be true of the other writer who associates Satan with jurisdiction over death, the author of Hebrews, who says that Jesus came to dismantle Satan's operation, to "set him aside" (24).

In the Gospel of John, Jesus has harsh words about Satan, calling him a homicide and liar from the beginning, in effect the begetter of all sinners, including the Judeans he is addressing (19). Most likely, Jesus is thinking of the first killer, Cain. He is certainly not referring to Satan as the metaphorical killer of Adam and Eve. This notion only came later (7, 12, 31). The connection to Cain is made explicit in 1 John, where Satan is designated as the father of Cain and all sinners. The author says that Jesus came to work against all of Satan's "works," referring to his enticements to sin (27).

I have objected to translating the Greek designation of Satan, *ho ponēros*, as "the Evil One" in the Gospels; but in 1 John it would certainly seem to be appropriate. Other New Testament authors agree in finding Satan sinful, and, furthermore, as deserving of punishment for his sins. This may be the meaning of Matthew's reference to the fire prepared for Devil and his angels (14), and it is certainly true of John the Divine when he destines him for the lake of fire (30). John the Evangelist may also have punishment in mind when he speaks of the ruler of this world as having been already judged or convicted (20).

As is evident, there are various viewpoints on Satan in the New Testament, but none of them are inconsistent with the Old Testament portrayal of him in the book of Job as God's assistant who sometimes oversteps his authority. We remember that God rebukes Satan for making Him go too far in testing Job, but then He lets Himself be talked into testing him further (3). In Zechariah, the Angel of Yahweh calls for Yahweh to rebuke Satan (4), as does the Archangel Michael in Jude (25), but there is no suggestion that these rebukes would lead to a "fall from heaven" any time soon! He remains, in effect, God's minister of justice throughout.

In sum, Satan comes off in the Bible as a highly dreaded and sinister figure. But the dread felt is not analogous to the fear of spies and infiltrators or terrorists from a foreign power or "evil empire" intent on undermining and destroying the entire state. Rather, it is akin to the unease and anxiety that comes from living in an oppressive local society where there is constant danger of being pulled over or audited or inspected or turned in or questioned or arraigned by suspicious and cynical or unscrupulous authorities; but still with hope that higher authorities can intervene for our benefit and relief. Hence the prayer suggested by the Lord: "Lead us not into temptation, but deliver us from evil."

Chapter 38

Belief in Satan

Now that we have seen the ways in which Satan is portrayed in the Bible, I have a *recommendation* and a *suggestion*.

*　*　*

The *recommendation* is that everyone should make a clear distinction between what is found in the Bible and what has been read back into the Bible from later unwarranted elaborations about Satan. This recommendation is particularly important for those readers of the Bible who believe that, because Satan is accepted as a real being by the authors of various books of the Bible, and especially because Jesus is recorded as treating Satan as real, they are obliged to believe in the existence of Satan as an article of faith. They should take care to believe in the Satan who is actually described and spoken about in the Bible, not the Satan who rebelled against God as Lucifer, and became God's enemy, or the Satan in the guise of a serpent who deceived Eve. They should believe in the Satan who, as a chief minister of God Himself, is shown to be responsible for testing the virtue of humankind, including Jesus.

In short, believing in the post-biblical Satan as if he were biblical falsifies the Bible and falsifies one's faith.

I need not explain at length the many ways in which Christianity changed because of spurious ideas of Satan: for instance, in helping to develop a harsh notion of the original sin of Adam and

Eve, by which Satan not only tricked them into sinning but also, in so doing, was given control over them and all of their descendants, with the right of imprisoning them and torturing them in hell. Instead of being seen as God's angel, concerned to protect Him from unscrupulous humans who only feign virtue, Satan became an active enemy of God whose only goal is to corrupt the virtue of humans and thereby deprive God of their company and deprive them of God for all eternity.

*   *   *

My *suggestion* is that, once existence has been firmly denied to the fantasized post-biblical Satan, we not concern ourselves very much about the real biblical Satan, whether he exists or not. That is, whether Satan is real or just part of the old Hebrew cosmos that can be set aside, or whether we think we are supposed to believe that he is real or not, there is not much practical benefit in worrying about him. For there is no clear way of determining whether Satan is actively putting enticements in our way or not, and we must meet all temptations in the same way: by rejecting them.

When Jesus taught his disciples, and us, how to pray, he left it unclear whether, after begging Our Father not to bring us into trials and temptations, we were to ask Him to deliver us simply from falling into sin, or to deliver us from Satan. Many biblical exegetes believe that he meant the latter; and, since these exegetes have had the wrong idea about Satan, considering him an enemy of God rather than God's assistant, they read the petition to mean, "Deliver us from the Super-Bad Evil One who wants to destroy us." But, now that we know what Satan is really like in the Bible, if we follow the personal interpretation of "evil," the petition means something like: "Please don't let your hard-nosed assistant carry out his plans to trip us up."

Fortunately, the Lord's Prayer in all or most vernacular translations has chosen the impersonal meaning, "Deliver us from what is bad," without worrying whether the bad comes straight from God or is mediated by Satan.

* * *

Another approach would be to take seriously what Jesus has to say about Satan. Although he acknowledges, in effect, that Satan was appointed to rule over the kingdoms of the world (Luke 4:5–8), he soon predicted that he would suffer a sudden fall from power (Luke 10:18). He also pointed out that Satan needed permission to undertake his testing (Luke 22:31–32). Finally, he said, speaking of his coming crucifixion, "Now will the ruler of this world be driven out" (John 12:31–33).

So, in the latter interpretation Satan's regimen was abolished with the institution of the New Covenant. All these centuries he was needlessly feared as the instigator of trials and tribulations. He is not the cause of any of the physical and moral evils that beset us. We must face up to realities: all of the moral deviations on our planet are due to ourselves, and it is our responsibility to try to eliminate them. As for physical ills, we must do everything in our power to ameliorate their effects upon us and our neighbors, with God's help.

* * *

A final word. The really bad Satan has been with us for much too long. It is high time to do justice to the real Satan, who was only moderately bad.

Scripture Index

John (*continued*)

6:68–71	81
7:3–4	80
7:6–8	81
8:12	85
8:31	78
8:44	79, 116
9:2–3	149
12:27–28	83
12:31–32	83–84
12:31–33	170
12:35	85
13:2	81
13:27	82
14:30–31	83
16:7–11	84, 96
17:15	85

Acts

5	77
5:1–10	72
9:1–22	72
10	77
10:38	71
13:6–11	72
22:3–15	72
26	77
26:12–18	72

Romans

3:9	146
3:24	146
5:12	146
5:12–21	47
5:18	147
16:20	45, 48

1 Corinthians

2:6–8	98
2:10	121
5:5	38, 94
6:3	38

7:5	39
10:5–10	39
10:13	40
13:11	103
15:22	47

2 Corinthians

2:4–9	41
2:11	42
2:17	43
4:3–4	42, 91
6:15	45
8:8	42
9:13	42
11:3	45, 47
11:13–14	43
11:15	43
12:7–9	43–44, 66
12:70–79	61
13:1–7	44

Galatians

1:8	49
6:1	49

Ephesians

1:19–21	99
2:1–2	99
2:6	99
3:1	99
3:10	99
3:14	99
4:1	99
4:17–18	100
4:25–26	100
6:10–17	100
6:20	99

Colossians

1:15	99
1:15–17	98

General Index